AN INSIDE LOOK AT

10

OF TODAY'S MOST

INNOVATIVE
CHURCHES

10

AN INSIDE LOOK AT

"The Church's future can be bright if it's willing to be spirit directed."

BILL HYBELS

OF TODAY'S MOST

INNOVATIVE CHURCHES

WHAT THEY'RE DOING, **HOW** THEY'RE DOING IT & **HOW YOU** CAN APPLY THEIR IDEAS IN YOUR CHURCH

ELMER L. TOWNS

Regal Books

A Division of GL Publications
Ventura, California, U.S.A.

Published by Regal Books
A Division of GL Publications
Ventura, California U.S.A.
Printed in U.S.A.

Library of Congress Cataloging-in-Publication Data   7/91

Towns, Elmer L.
            10 of today's most innovative churches: what they're doing, how they're doing it &
            how you can apply their ideas in your church / Elmer Towns.
                    p. cm.
            ISBN 0-8308-1405-7
            1. Church renewal—United States—Case studies. 2. Church
management—Case studies. I. Title.
BT91.T68 1990
254'.00973—dc20   90-46640
                                                                                      CIP

All photographs used with permission.

1 2 3 4 5 6 7 8 9 10 / KP / X3.0 / 95 94 93 92 91

Rights for publishing this book in other languages are contracted by Gospel Literature International (GLINT) foundation. GLINT also provides technical help for the adaptation, translation, and publishing of Bible study resources and books in scores of languages worldwide. For further information, contact GLINT, Post Office Box 488, Rosemead, California, 91770, U.S.A., or the publisher.

CONTENTS

ANALYSIS:
Elements of Innovation for Today's Churches

PREFACE

Dr. Elmer Towns

I WAS LECTURING IN BURBANK, CALIFORNIA, ON THE CHANGE NEEDED FOR churches to meet the challenge of the twenty-first century. Bill Greig, Jr., a friend for 30 years, sent me a note: "Will you write a book on how a church can change the methods that need changing?" I was flattered because Bill is president of Gospel Light Publications and Regal Books. I phoned him the next weekend. "Bill," I said, "people won't read a book telling churches to change. It'll just be my opinion against theirs."

Being a successful publisher, Bill agreed with me. People laugh at the "We've never done it that way before" syndrome, but it's real. A theoretical book on change will not change churches.

"Let me paint 10 portraits and hang them up for people to see," I countered to Bill, in a phone call. "Each portrait will be a story of a church that has successfully changed. The credibility of 10 churches will make the book about change believable. Their stories will be 10 persuasive arguments for innovation or change." This book is the result of that phone call.

In 1969 I wrote *The Ten Largest Sunday Schools and What Makes Them Grow*, featuring 10 model churches. When the book was published, over 20 years ago now, most people thought the American church was ineffective and dying. This revolutionary book told about exciting churches that had made an impact on their community. Its thesis was that these 10 churches were getting the job done because they hadn't changed. They effectively applied traditional methods of growth. The book hit the church market like a thunderclap, becoming an instant best-seller. The 10 churches became role models for a generation of church growth.

Now, 20 years later, I am writing another book on 10 churches to feature growth by innovative methods. This book will focus on churches that are pacesetters for the twenty-first century. Whereas the first book looked at past methods, this volume focuses on the future, and on new ideas for ministry in the twenty-first century.

I had asked a number of friends to suggest the most innovative church they knew. I began with a list of 25, and started writing and visiting churches. Some were eliminated because their innovative methods were similar to other churches described in this book. Some innovative methods were not producing fruit, and others were not biblical.

The 10 churches in this book are all different, yet each has a message for us. I tried to choose different sections of the country, but there are two churches from both Atlanta and San Diego. I couldn't omit any of these because all are outstanding. I also tried to choose churches of different doctrinal stances, different sizes, different views of sanctification and different emphases on methods. At times the diversity of these churches frankly contradict the totalitarian attitude of those who believe that their method is the only way to do ministry. This just shows that the God of heaven must laugh at our narrowness, and that He often uses those who disagree with our particular bias.

Five areas of change are greatly influencing current church growth. These five factors are evident to some degree in each of the 10 churches in this book:

First, they have created innovative methods based on research. They are able to target a receptive audience because they have a profile of who they can reach (see chapter 15). I call this "reaching the reachable."

Second, these are "Boomer" churches—churches that have especially targeted Baby Boomers, the generation born between 1946 and 1964. Several have adopted new programs specifically to reach the Boomers (see chapter 11). Within 10 years the larger Church will be a Boomer church that will influence the culture. Those who ignore or reject the Boomers will become hibernating churches. America will be run by Boomers within 10 years, and the church must be prepared for their style of leadership.

Third, these 10 churches exercise an effective style of pastoral leadership that is different from traditional leadership.

Fourth, these churches are innovative in worship expression, refusing to be tied to the worship forms of the past (chapter 12).

Finally, these churches are consumer oriented. They understand marketing. In short, they not only can preach, teach, counsel and evangelize; they can run a church in a business-like manner—without becoming a business. The Church of the future will be more influenced by business methods than ever before, rather than following traditional ecclesiastical styles of operation.

Churches Never Change—Or Do They?

This book on 10 innovative churches and how their programs impact their community demonstrates that churches can develop exciting programs that change the lives of members and the community. These model churches are committed to the fundamentals of the faith. Unchanged in doctrine, they still seek innovative methods to meet the floating needs of culture. The author's assumption is that doctrine and principles never change. They are eternal. The doctrine of the substitutionary atonement or the principle of evangelization for all people will always be the same, because principles are eternal.

But the way we apply our principles to different cultures does change, because culture changes. While the principle of evangelism does not change, we must adopt innovative evangelistic methods and adapt them to the times. An American revival meeting is an illustration of adapting an eternal principle to a culture that is constantly changing. These 10 churches are great soul-winning churches because they are committed to the eternal principle of evangelism, while not relying on the fall and spring revival meetings as their method of evangelism. They have adopted new soul-winning methods to get the job done.

Our culture is like a drag racer, rushing toward the future. But will the church be left behind? Too many congregations are hibernating churches, withdrawing from the world, refusing to meet the challenge of society. When the kids walk into their services they groan, "This is history." Many churches are not keeping up, but falling behind. To listen to their pastors, they don't want to keep up. They want to hibernate until the rapture.

These 10 high-impact churches design innovative programs to influence their culture. They are characterized by five principles. First, they know where people are in their thinking and life-style, and they know how to reach them. Second, they create innovative programs and use new techniques to reach people. Third, they are not tied to old programs that no longer work. Fourth, they are not afraid to change; they are flexible in method, though not with the gospel message. Fifth, they demonstrate a flair for developing new programs. Like the sizzle of a steak, they attract people, create an appetite for a solution and make Christianity enjoyable. People seem to enjoy worshiping and serving in these churches.

When the Boomers Take Over

We have said that these 10 "change-driven" churches either recognize or are driven by the values of the Boomer generation also. The growing impact of the Boomer generation deserves a further word.

The Boomers' values are different from those of people born in the Depression or during World War II. Boomers are optimistic, technological, "now" oriented and winners. At one time they were the Pepsi generation. Like it or not, within 10 years the Boomers will take over our churches. At this writing they are junior executives, not yet sitting in the executive offices. They do not dominate the board rooms, control our denominations nor, with a few exceptions, pastor our largest churches. But within 10 years Boomers will emerge in the decision-making positions of leadership. They will run our country and our churches.

Boomers march to a different drumbeat, and express their values in their own way. Previous generations have been influenced by their elders, but not the Boomers. They have retained their uniqueness as they move into maturity. This book will help churches prepare for the coming Boomer takeover. Predicting the future here is not mystical, like reading tea leaves or gazing into a crystal ball. If we know how the Boomers live now, how they serve God and worship, then we will understand how the Church will function in the twenty-first century.

Pastors Are Generals, Not Red Cross Workers

John Maxwell, pastor of Skyline Wesleyan Church in greater San Diego, California, describes the senior pastor of the future as a general who directs an army, not a Red Cross worker helping the wounded one at a time. The general leads his army by delegating different tasks to staff officers. One staff member is responsible for artillery, and others for tanks and the infantry. There is a medical officer who has the responsibility of caring for the wounded. Maxwell says too many pastors stop to tend to one wounded soldier when they are supposed to lead the army. They stop the battle, leaving the troops without a leader—and the battle is lost. One can see a column of tanks waiting while a general puts bandages on a wounded soldier—and in the meantime other soldiers die because they do not have a leader. The pastor/general must give effective leadership so that no hurting person in his church is overlooked. But at the same time he must provide leadership for every aspect of the battle. The pastor/general wins the battle through his staff officers.

The pastor should not be merely a leader of people but a leader of leaders. The Church of the future will see a different style of pastoral leadership. The pastor will not be a dictator, but will train his board and staff to minister, deploy his board and staff for ministry and evaluate their effectiveness.

Whereas pastors used to lead people, today's pastor is training leaders (lay and staff) who in turn lead the church. The old question was: Who is in control—the pastor or the board? The 10 churches described here are neither board-controlled nor pastor-controlled. The new question: Who is leading the church? is not about control, but leadership.

These 10 churches are not just buildings, assets, people or programs. They are task-oriented, driven by the the Great Commission and measuring the effectiveness of their ministry by that objective. There is accountability when money is spent and programs are finished. Many churches waste millions on programs that are ineffective, buildings that are nonfunctional and tasks that are nonproductive. The key to effective church growth is leadership—effective team leadership that emphasizes shared goal-setting, shared problem-solving and shared decision-making.

Good pastoral leadership is not a dictatorship. It is not what the pastor does *to* people but what he does *with* people that makes effective church leadership. Pastoral leadership is plural. It is pastor *and* people, shepherd and sheep, the leader and the led. The key to leadership is followership. The successful pastorate is not measured by how many listen to the pastor preach. It is measured by how many follow His leadership in ministry, evangelism or caring for people.

Different Worship that Is the Same

These 10 churches have worship styles that are different from each other, and different from other churches in their neighborhood. Several of them worship differently than they did a few years ago. They have changed to meet the needs of worshipers. They have changed the time of worship, the order of service, the type of music, the style of preaching, the audience participation and even the place of worship.

Going to a new form of worship is not always easy. In the past, doctrinal diversity seemed to be the great source of religious controversy. Christians argued over the form of baptism, Calvinism vs. Arminianism and when the rapture would occur. The Boomers seem to be tolerant of doctrinal disagreements but are deeply opinionated about worship forms. (Boomers are into form and function; doctrine is about third on their list of church priorities.) Now people argue the virtues of a Bible teaching church vs. a renewal service with praise choruses.

Which is right? Pastors are fired when they change the form of worship. Churches split over forms of worship. The greatest revolution in the modern church—forms of worship—is also the source of the greatest controversy.

The churches portrayed here have something to say to the American church scene about worship. Jack Hayford says that what we have is more than a *change* in worship, it's a reformation. These 10 churches have reformed the form of worship but not its object. God is worshiped in their services. If we could all focus on the One who is worshiped, rather than on our words or posture when we worship, we would realize that the more worship changes the more it stays the same.

The Church as a Consumer-Oriented Business

These 10 churches are not tied to the traditional way churches operate, with the pastor ministering and the people sitting on boards or committees to actually run the church. These churches have reversed the procedure. The pastor gives leadership (he runs the church), and the lay people minister. This is revolutionary, but a revolution worth dying for. The greatest asset of these 10 churches is the vast percentage of lay people that have been involved in ministry and/or pastoral care of the flock.

Years ago I began to talk about what a seminary did not teach a pastor. Pastors were taught evangelism, preaching, teaching and counseling. They were taught to minister, but not to lead a church. Seminaries did not teach pastors how to train people, delegate, organize and manage a church. The seminaries did a poor job in equipping pastors as leaders.

The Church of the future will be run like a business, it will be business-like in its organization and administration, but at its best the Church will not be a business. The pastor, like the president of a business, will be a manager, which is another way to describe leadership.

The future-oriented Church will be consumer oriented, which means it must understand and follow marketing principles. The business world has adopted "niche-marketing," meaning that they identify a need, design a product to service the need and advertise the product to those who need it. No business can afford to advertise every product to the entire public. A business must find a niche and service that market.

The Church has spent millions on advertising to the general public, perhaps because the gospel must be presented to all people (Matt. 28:19, 20; Mark 16:15). But a local church must realize that it has limited resources and limited time. A church does not have unlimited resources, and it will not and cannot reach all people. It must exercise priorities in carrying out ministry. This means that a church must budget expenditures so it can focus on reaching those it can evangelize effectively and efficiently. A church must find its niche in the neighborhood and reach the reachable.

A church cannot spend thousands or millions on general television advertisements for the gospel. It doesn't have the money, and even if it did it could not effectively service the response of a general audience. The local church of the future must know its neighborhood (do market research), its target person (develop a prospect profile), the method that will reach those who are responsive-receptive people (through media research) and it must then reach the reachable (advertise).

Since Boomers emphasize form and function, the local church must give attention to excellence in its *form* of worship and the way it does business. It must also make sure that the message of the gospel will *function* in the life of the parishioner.

This will be a controversial book because it talks about change and gives credibility to new forms and functions. If this book makes people think about the future it will have accomplished half its goal. If it makes people change their old methods for new and workable ones, it will have gone the second mile. If it convinces people not to change the fundamentals of the faith but to use innovative methods to reach lost people with the gospel, it will have accomplished its goal.

Diversity of ministry is the buzz word for the twenty-first century. These 10 churches are meeting the future challenge, but doing it in different ways. At times they conflict in their strategy (anti-choir vs. utilization of the choir). They are different in doctrine (Calvinistic vs. Arminian), different in views of sanctification

(Pentecostal vs. Baptist), different in worship forms and they have different purposes for small group ministry. They are different in socioeconomic levels, age-concentration and Walrath City Church types. But in spite of their diversity they agree on the essentials of the faith. They agree on the goal of reaching people for Christ. They agree that believers should be bonded to a local church and live godly lives.

I have not said everything that might be said about these churches. They have weak areas that are not discussed. This is not an expose; my focus has been on their innovative programs. I don't recommend everything these churches do, and I don't agree with everything I've written. I've tried to describe each church honestly, without pejorative language, as they have told me their stories. Even though I have written descriptively and not norma-tively, I respect their overall ministry for Christ, and I count them as my friends. They are doing many programs the right way. They will become model churches as they move toward the twenty-first century. Let us learn from them.

My thanks to all who have helped to make this book possible. I could not have written it without the help of the pastors, staff and secretaries of these churches. I could not have written it with-out the help of my staff at Liberty University and the Church Growth Institute at Lynchburg, Virginia. Special recognition goes to Mrs. Judy Forlano, who coordinated my travel to these church-es, gathered facts for the chart at the back of the book and worked with the pastor of each church as he proofread his chapter to veri-fy its contents.

While many have helped in this project, I take full responsibili-ty for all weaknesses and mistakes. May God use it to cause thou-sands of churches to grow like the 10 portrayed on these pages.

ELMER TOWNS
Lynchburg, Virginia
Summer, 1990

1

MANAGING CHANGE FOR CHURCH GROWTH

Skyline Wesleyan Church
San Diego, California

Dr. John Maxwell, Pastor

SKYLINE WESLEYAN CHURCH IS ONE OF THE MOST INNOVATIVE CHURCH-es in America because its pastor, John Maxwell, is the personi-fication of a change agent and trendsetter. Though other churches are changing, too, Skyline is changing more efficiently and effec-tively because of Maxwell's effectiveness as a manager for change.

I am also highlighting Skyline because Maxwell demonstrates the fact that effective change can happen anywhere. While he ministers in California—the nation's trendsetter in clothes, enter-tainment, food and community planning—he is not a native Cali-fornian. He grew up in a traditional small town in central Ohio, and his roots were in a small denomination that has exhibited little innovation. He graduated from Circleville Bible College, a tradi-tional Bible school of approximately 150 students.

The innovative programs and vision of the California scene were already present in embryonic form in the ministry of young Maxwell in his first two pastorates. He led Faith Memorial Church in Lancaster, Ohio, from 385 in attendance to over 1,400 in weekly attendance. In a small town of 28,000 population, Maxwell built a 1,700 seat sanctuary.

But numbers alone do not necessarily indicate an innovative program. The Lancaster church used evangelistic busing methods to build attendance, but young Maxwell, age 28 at the time, went further. He organized a free, citywide bus service for the elderly in conjunction with the monthly arrival of social security checks. The town, which had previously had no bus service, rallied with bus benches. The newspaper provided free advertisement to inform people of the bus schedule. The business community loved the idea. When Maxwell walked into a city council meeting to receive an award, the room rose in applause. Such was an indication of the future of church innovations when Maxwell arrived in San Diego in 1981.

Background and Growth Pattern

The Skyline Wesleyan Church of San Diego was founded by Orville Butcher in 1947. It became the largest Wesleyan church in the world. Butcher was a great pastor who produced an outstanding music program and, during the busing boom of the early '70s, led the church to over 1,000 in attendance. But the busing surge declined in the '80s and the bus program was dropped at Skyline. When Maxwell became the pastor, weekly attendance averaged approximately 1,000.

A Decade of Growth

Under Maxwell's leadership, attendance took off. Within nine years attendance has grown to a weekly average of over 3,500. The weekly offering is $55,000, and the annual budget is $3.5 million. Maxwell has led the church from one morning worship service to three (plus a Spanish service), and from one Sunday School to three (8 A.M., 9:30 A.M. and 11 A.M.). Wednesday evening attendance has grown from 150 to over 1,300. The church has raised $3 million in cash toward a new location, and has pledged $7 million over and above regular giving for the new building.

But growth in buildings, money and property are not the sole indicators of what makes this church effective. Other indications are the fact that 50 percent of its people are involved in ministry; lives have been changed; and workable ideas have been channeled to other churches through Injoy Ministry, a corporation that packages the ideas of Maxwell for other congregations across America. These ideas are also communicated through conferences held by Maxwell through GRADE ministries, and the Charles E. Fuller Evangelistic Association (Breaking the 200 Barrier, etc.).

The GRADE program is designed to involve all church members in outreach, each person using his or her unique spiritual gift. Maxwell calls those with the gift of evangelism "Andrews." They are involved in soul winning. "Timothys" have the gift of teaching new converts. Those with the gift of showing mercy are "Barnabases." They make pastoral calls to absentees, the sick, shut-ins and those with problems. The "Abrahams" are intercessors who pray for the outreach programs.

Many men not involved elsewhere in the church's ministry are enlisted as the Pastor's Prayer Partners. Maxwell meets with his 100 Prayer Partners once a month on Saturday morning for prayer and discipleship training. The men are divided into four teams, and each Sunday a different team meets with Maxwell for prayer before the first worship service. About 20 men gather around the pastor as he kneels; each man lays hands on Maxwell and prays for him. Then during each morning service the group of men gather in a room above the pulpit to intercede while Maxwell is preaching. After the service, the men come down to the auditorium to see what God has done through their prayer.

Maxwell the Man

"Hi, I'm John and I pastor a traditional church," Maxwell said as he introduced himself to a church growth seminar sponsored by Fuller Theological Seminary. Two things about that statement invite analysis. First, Skyline Wesleyan Church is not a traditional church by American standards. It is innovative in attitude, scheduling, preaching techniques and vision.

The second thing to note is that John Maxwell introduces himself as "John." Most American pastors want to be called by their title. But John is an unusual pastor, and his unusual results come from within rather than from titles and other externals.

One of Maxwell's strongest traits is his ability to attract and lead his staff. The pastoral staff at Skyline may be the best gathering of associate pastors in the country—not because any one of them is individually superior when compared to other outstanding assistant pastors, but because, as a team led by Maxwell, they synergistically produce a ministry of superior quality.

Spiritual Foundations of a Change Agent

John Maxwell is an exemplary church change agent because he understands the managerial dynamics of change. He also knows the internal necessities for innovation because he has experienced them.

Five Life-changing Experiences

Maxwell says that God stretched him and changed him with five crucial experiences. The principles by which he now lives were hammered out on the anvil of five crises.

The death of a friend—and of a habit. The first crisis was in the early '70s, a time of spiritual formation early in Maxwell's ministry. The death of a friend changed him from a happy-go-lucky preacher who wanted to be a friend to everyone, into a driven man of God.

At the time, Maxwell was with his first church, in Hillhan, Indiana. He began with seven people, and although he moved the congregation forward dramatically in terms of numbers, he says it was not growing spiritually. During this time, Maxwell visited a friend in the hospital repeatedly. Looking back, he confesses that one of his main drives was to get the patient to like him. Then the friend died. During the funeral Maxwell wept openly— not for the grieving family or friends, but for his own barren spiritual condition.

Over the next year John earnestly sought the Lord, repenting of his own spiritual callousness. He remembers one Saturday night when he was preparing for a sermon. He was lying under the dining room table, praying with his face to the floor and begging God for true spiritual power. It was not one instantaneous moment that changed his life; but gradually, over a period of months he became more committed to the spiritual dynamics of pastoring a flock. Like John Wesley, Maxwell obtained perfect love and true holiness. He testifies that he was filled with the Holy Spirit and received power for spiritual witnessing to lead people to Christ.

Expanding horizons. A second crisis experience happened in February, 1973, at a bus conference in Lynchburg, Virginia. Up to this point, because of his ecclesiastical background, Maxwell had not been exposed to great evangelistic churches or great evangelistic preaching. At Lynchburg, though, he saw the great busing ministry at Thomas Road Baptist Church. He heard the testimonies of leaders from massive churches with tremendous evangelistic outreaches. He realized he had limited God by his own unbelief. Under the ministry of Wally Beebe, Jerry Falwell, Bob Gray and others, Maxwell testifies, "I realized that I needed to expand my horizons."

Back in his room at the Holiday Inn, he wrestled with God all night. Lying on the floor again, Maxwell made a commitment to double his church in Lancaster in one year. He was averaging 400 in attendance, and he determined to have an additional 400 on the buses within one year. He also committed to go back and publicly announce his new determination to his church.

Upon returning to Ohio, he rallied the people to begin the following Saturday knocking on doors to invite people to ride a bus to Sunday School. On Sunday morning the bus pulled up to the church and 19 children got off. John remembers hugging everyone in the church foyer as they counted the children. "Since we had 19 children on the bus," he announced, "we can use our other bus and get 38 next Sunday." And they did. Within a year they had reached their goal of averaging as many on the buses as in worship attendance. Maxwell testifies, "When I began to think big and not limit God, the people began to think big and not limit God."

The barren altar. The third crisis happened in November, 1973, at a Sword of the Lord conference under the ministry of John R. Rice. Maxwell was convicted about the "barren altar"—the lack of conversions at his church. He wrestled with God in the car all the way home. He prayed, "Lord let there never be a Sunday when people are not saved at the church." Big attendance was not enough. Upon his return, he again announced to his congregation that in the following year he would do all he could not to have a barren altar, but to make it a great year of soul-winning.

During that year, Maxwell invited me to preach for him at the church. Since it was the weekend of our wedding anniversary, he invited me to bring my wife, saying that we would go out for our

---

Leaders are learners. Until a leader learns the eternal laws of change, he cannot produce it in others.

---

anniversary dinner. When we arrived, however, John told us that it was visitation night, and he had made a commitment to go soul-winning. Even though there was social pressure on him to keep his commitment to me, that evening Maxwell visited a lawyer named John Polston and won him to the Lord. For the next several years when I visited the church to preach, Polston would remind me how happy he was that Maxwell had gone soul-winning that night instead of going out for an anniversary dinner.

In 1974 Maxwell made a goal to personally win 200 people to Christ. A great sense of revival broke out among the people when he made that announcement. He did not quite reach his goal that year, but he did lead 186 to pray to receive Christ. He feels that this established the credibility of soul-winning among the church members, and established the foundation for all of the changes in the church, including constructing new buildings and instituting new ministries.

Networking and praying. The fourth experience was not so much a crisis as it was a number of rich conversations with successful pastors. Maxwell phoned several great pastors and offered them $100 each for an hour of their time in order to discover the reasons why their churches had done so well. As he visited and talked with these outstanding leaders, he asked them to pray with him. And after each interview he went to his car, bowed his head over the steering wheel and asked for spiritual strength to build a great church.

A crisis of glory. The fifth experience occurred when Maxwell received the award for having the fastest-growing Sunday School in Ohio in 1976. The award, a large banner, was presented by *Christian Life* magazine at the International Christian Education Convention in Detroit, Michigan. The Sunday School at the Lancaster church had grown from an average attendance of 860 to 1,012.

After the award ceremony, Maxwell returned to his hotel and, again lying on his face, laid the banner out before God. At that moment he realized that he had been honored for doing only what he *should* do, for growth was what every church *ought* to do. He opened the Scriptures and reread the words of Jesus in Matthew 16:18: "I will build my church." The church belonged to Jesus, not to John Maxwell. It is God who is to be honored, not men. In the midst of this crisis, Maxwell recalls, he decided to give God the glory for everything in his ministry. That night he realized he was gifted to serve the Lord, and that God must get the credit for any gift because "Every good...gift is from above" (Jas. 1:17).

Leadership Qualities

Maxwell believes you don't change your church; you change your leader. He agrees with Rick Warren, pastor of Saddleback Community Church in Mission Viejo, California, who says, "Leaders are learners." Until a leader learns the eternal laws of change, he cannot produce it in others.

In order to lead people to change, Maxwell believes, a leader must first make a commitment to God. Second, the commitment must be made public. And third, the leader must make a commitment to his or her followers.

Maxwell says, "At the end of a public declaration to my people, I found they were willing to follow me in change." He likes to go to the altar and invite his people to come pray with him. He says, "People are looking for a leader, and change begins with the leader." People will not change unless they see the leader's sincerity, feel his commitment to God and know in their hearts that this is what God wants them to do.

Principles of Change

Growth as Change

Growth equals change, Maxwell explains, because you cannot grow *unless* you change. Yet, standing before his pastoral staff, he reminded them that the opposite is not true: "All change is not growth, because many people change things not for the better but for the worse." In his Injoy Life tape club, designed for training people in leadership, he notes that "All change does not represent progress, but if we do not change there will be no progress."

"Change is the price we pay for growth," Maxwell says. He knows that many people in his church want progress. They want a new building, they desire outreach success, and want to grow in Jesus Christ; but many do not want change. Therefore, Maxwell knows that a church growth pastor must be a change agent.

Truths About Change

As Maxwell faced his new pastorate at Skyline in 1981, he knew he had to turn the attendance around. He knew that he was pro-change, although he was not sure about the people. And he knew three things about change.

First, as he announced to the pastoral staff, "We live in an era of change." Maxwell knew that everyone was changing in several areas of their lives. The Skyline neighborhood itself was changing. People were moving out and the church faced a crisis. He knew he could not have a status-quo ministry or rest on the past reputation of the church.

Second, Maxwell knew that people look to a leader in an era of change. The challenge facing the pastors was to lead people to apply familiar principles of change to their worship and ministry styles, without changing their commitment to eternal truth.

In the third place, Maxwell knew that the effectiveness of his church's ministry would depend on the response of the people to

---

All change does not represent progress, but if we do not change there will be no progress.

---

the way the pastoral leaders tried to lead them through change. He announced to his staff, "Our ability to successfully change and bring it about in others will determine our success as leaders."

Maxwell likes the term "yeasty" used by John Naisbitt in his book, *Megatrends*. To Maxwell, the word "yeasty" describes the era of change in which we are living, a "time between two ages"—the fading industrial era and the coming information-processing era. "This yeasty time is filled with opportunities to do more for God than we have ever done before," he says.

Since Maxwell is an optimist, he does not see change as a threat, but as a great platform on which progress can be made. He warns against the "plateau" mentality that can inhibit this progress. Many congregations have experienced a surge of growth—usually brought about by an innovative method, a new staff member or new enthusiasm for an old program—only to settle down at a stagnant plateau. Once a church has plateaued, the people may lose the open attitude toward change that is necessary to keep the church in a continual growth mode. When churches run out of new ideas or new programs, they stop growing.

The problem is compounded, Maxwell says, because many pastors tenaciously hold on to the methods that first brought about growth and refuse to look for newer methods as the old ones grow stale or as culture changes. As an illustration, many churches exploded in growth during the '70s with evangelistic busing. We have already seen that Maxwell's church in Lancaster, Ohio, grew from 400 to over 1,000 in the mid-1970s, primarily because of the bus ministry. But when Maxwell went to California busing was dying, if not already dead, so he did not attempt to lead the church into an aggressive bus ministry.

One of Maxwell's strengths is his ability to change with the times and update his methods, while never changing the principles of ministry.

Three Essential Attitudes of Change

Maxwell says leaders must have three attitudes toward change. First, they must realize that the future will not be like the past. Maxwell is a believer in the ultimate potential of people for change and innovation. As an illustration, he points out that while dogs have dug holes with their paws for thousands of years, man, who used to dig holes with a shovel, now has a backhoe.

Second, Maxwell says leaders must realize that the future will not be like what they expect; change is coming so fast that few changes will turn out the way we project. Yet, Maxwell says, "We must embrace change as a friend."

A third essential, he stresses, is to realize that the rate of change will be faster than in the past. Today's typical college student will have to be retrained three times for different vocational objectives before he dies. He will work at 30 different companies before he retires, simply because the world is changing. Maxwell points out that 100 years ago 50 percent of America's work force was involved in agriculture. Today, only 2 percent work on the farm.

Why People Resist Change

One of John Maxwell's favorite stories is about the New Yorker who was celebrating his hundredth birthday. A reporter interviewed him and said, "I'll bet you have seen a lot of changes in your life!"

"Yes," the man said, "and I've been against every one of them."

To be good change agents, John feels that church leaders must know why people resist change, and develop a strategy that incorporates them into the process of change. Being able to answer his opponents helps explain why he has been successful in accomplishing so many changes in his own ministry. He understands the reasons why people resist change:

First, people resist change because of *misunderstanding*. "When people do not understand why they should change, they will work to oppose it," Maxwell says.

Second, people oppose change because of *lack of ownership*. When church members are not involved in the change process, they resist any new thing being pushed on them. When Maxwell introduces a new program, he involves as many people as possible in the vision, plans and implementation. When people are not given ownership in a new idea, they will fight it.

Third, people don't like to get out of *habit patterns*. They may resist a new program or method because it would change the routine with which they are comfortable. People are habit prone, so they fight anything that is different.

Fourth, people may feel that *change is not worth the price*. The reward for changing may appear too small. Since people know that change is costly, they want to get something in exchange for their sacrifice. If the reward is inadequate for the effort, they will resist change.

Fifth, people resist change when they are threatened with *the loss of something that is valuable* to them. People resist change most when they feel they are losing security, money or control.

Sixth, the *"satisfaction factor"* explains why people resist change. They are basically satisfied with the old ways and they don't want to change.

Seventh, another reason is *a negative attitude toward change in general.* Some people's entire thought process is based on the idea that nothing should be changed.

Eighth, people resist change when there is *a lack of respect for the leader.* Unless the followers trust the leaders, they will feel so uncomfortable with change that they will fight it.

Finally, *tradition* is the ninth reason why people fight change. The attitude is, "We've never done it that way before."

A Formula for Change

John Maxwell has a formula for change that he repeats at staff meetings and in sermons. By restating it frequently he is creating an atmosphere where change is expected. As a matter of fact, if things don't change around Skyline, people wonder what's wrong.

The Maxwell Formula for Change

People change when they:
- Hurt enough that they have to change;
- Learn enough that they want to change;
- Receive enough that they are able to change.

The first part of the formula deals with negative motivation. When people hurt enough, the need to change can overpower tradition, negative attitudes and habit patterns. Maxwell often says that when the pain to remain the same is greater than the pain to change, then people will make adjustments. He tells his staff that unless people are uncomfortable with the old, they will not be comfortable with the new.

Maxwell laughs when he tells the story of a man who refused to sign up for a hospitalization policy because it was against his principles. But when the boss threatened to fire him, the man immediately signed the policy. When asked why, he said, "The boss never explained it like that before."

The second step of Maxwell's formula—people will change when they learn enough—involves education. Maxwell feels that a change agent has to be an educator who will lead people to see the goal of ministry, teach them how to have a more effective ministry and give them practical techniques to get there.

The third part of the formula involves giving people the strength to change. Maxwell notes that people will become innovative when they have the strength, vision, motivation and tools required to make a change. Therefore, the change agent must provide these strengths before asking people to change.

Ingredients for Success as a Change Agent

Maxwell believes the ability of a pastor to lead his church to change is the best predictor of success. If a pastor cannot successfully get people to change, then any new additions will probably not remain with the church and attendance will go back down when the pastor leaves. New members need new ministry and expanded programs. New members mean schedules must be expanded and space reallocated.

Exerting this kind of leadership is not easy. Maxwell reads the following statement from one of his Injoy lessons to his staff:

There is nothing more difficult to take in hand,

more perilous to conduct, or more uncertain in its
success, than to take the lead in the introduction of
a new order of things, because the innovator has
for enemies all those who have been under the old
conditions and only lukewarm defenders and those
who may do well under the new.

Therefore, Maxwell says, to bring about change in people's
lives is the highest test of leadership. He suggests that there are
five ingredients in the ministry of a successful change agent.

First, Maxwell says, *be open to change yourself*. Before we can
change others we have to be willing to change ourselves. To the
pastor who asks, "How can I change my church?" Maxwell has a
ready response: "First change yourself." Don't change churches or
marriages or people, he says, just change yourself and you will
lead people differently. Then they will change. In one of his sermons on change is the introductory statement, "Change: What will
you do with it—or what will it do with you?"

Second, *create an atmosphere of trust*. The more people trust
you as a leader the more they will change, Maxwell says. Many
times the people do not oppose change, but they oppose the
leader who is suggesting the change—because they do not trust
the leader. Even when people do not understand or agree with the
suggested change, they will often accept it anyway if they trust the
leader.

In 1984 Skyline Wesleyan Church was looking at 30 acres
called the Kenwood property for its new campus. Many people
came to a business meeting expecting to vote on the property.
After looking at the real estate and praying about it, the board
thought it was not the best location for the church. Maxwell
agreed with the board. Together they went to the meeting and
told the people that it wasn't the best property for relocation.
Unknown to Maxwell, many were against the site for various reasons. Yet they came and said they would have voted for the prop-

Skyline Wesleyan Church, San Diego, California

erty if the board and John recommended it. When they learned that John and the board disapproved of the property also, they gained even more trust in their leadership.

Previous *success* is a third ingredient that helps a leader encourage change. The more success the leader and the organization has, the more likely it will be for people to follow the leader in times of change. John uses the phrase, "A leader has to get a few wins under his belt"—comparing the minister with a new football coach who must win a few victories to earn the respect of his players. The pastor must have some previous successes before the people will follow him in a new venture of change.

Maxwell points out that many small victories win a leader the trust of the people when larger decisions arise. He illustrates this truth with the story of David and Goliath. Young David claimed that since he had been successful in defeating the bear and lion, he could defeat Goliath. John states, "Success breeds a climate for people to change." The opposite is also true: Failure in a leader breeds a climate in which people don't want to follow you.

Maxwell's fourth ingredient is *confidence.* The leader who has confidence can be a change agent because people will follow a confident leader. When a leader does not have confidence in what he is doing, people know it. They not only are reluctant to follow him, but resist him and any changes he suggests.

The fifth ingredient is *the openness to admit mistakes.* Why must a change agent be open to admitting failure? Because in all changes there is some degree of failure, John says. A good leader should honestly tell people where he has failed in the past. When the people realize that he is willing to admit failure, but that he has a healthy attitude and is willing to try again, they will follow.

In 1984 Maxwell began a cell-group program called Care Circles, thinking they would be a great outreach for Christ. Within six months there were only a few struggling, anemic groups. He had to shut them down. He had to be willing to look at the problem, tell the people why he failed and even to laugh about it. But the most important thing was to redirect the church and begin the idea of cells with a new strategy and new strength.

A Strategy for Ministry and Change

It takes more than a good attitude and desire to effect change. There must be a good strategy for change. John Maxwell illustrates his favorite strategy with five circles, like the waves that form when a rock is thrown into a pond. It is a good strategy for changing anything, whether in the church or in business.

The waves closest to the center are the highest. They are like the pastor or other change agent who is at the center and makes the biggest splash. Then the change agent works in each of the circles, beginning with the closest and most influential, taking care to adjust his or her methods according to the nature of each group.

Maxwell emphasizes that this strategy is not primarily to effect change, but to minister to each circle of people. The emphasis is on ministry—before change, during change and after change. Ministers who work through the circles with this motive can effectively lead a church to change.

Circle 1: The Change Agent

"The inner circle is myself," Maxwell says. Change doesn't begin with the congregation, but with the pastor. Maxwell asks himself five questions before trying to change something in his church.

1. Is this idea mine or God's?

2. John asks himself: Am I willing to pay the price this change will require? John says he has no difficulty discovering the will of God, but he does have difficulty with the price he needs to pay for the change. As he faced the relocation of the church, he wrestled with the price he would have to pay. John knew that if he led the church to move, he was making a five- to ten-year commitment of his life. He could not lead the people to move, then leave them for another church halfway through the project. To lead the church to a different location, he had to pay the price of long-term commitment.

3. John asks Whom will I lose? John realizes that with every change you will lose someone. There is no such thing as a change that makes everyone happy. Some pastors are willing to lead their church to change until they reach this point. Often, they are paralyzed because they are not willing to lose anyone.

4. How long will it take?

5. Will I be around after the change is made? If a pastor doesn't make the change properly, the church will get rid of him and call in someone else.

If a pastor can't give the right answer to these questions, the change should not be made. Why? Because change causes friction, John says. If these questions aren't settled satisfactorily, the leader will also be unsettled when the inevitable friction comes against him, his program and his family. After this process is completed, John Maxwell agrees with Jerry Falwell, who says, "Make a decision and make it work."

Once a pastor heard John talk about change and said, "I wish I had the principles of leadership that you have. I need an anchor to give me direction in my ministry. But the problem is I am blown about by the winds of other people's ideas."

A leader must answer these five questions with integrity before he moves to the second circle, John adds. The probability of success for change is determined in circle number one. Bold leadership is essential. "People follow a convictional leader, not a confused one," Maxwell says.

Circle 2: The Main Person

After the leader is sure of himself, the next focus is on what Maxwell calls "the main person." When a pastor enters this second circle he is looking for input. The main person is the individual who is responsible for the area to be changed. This could be the chairperson of the committee, a minister of education, or a Sunday School superintendent. It is essential to get to this person quickly, gather as much data as possible, and catch his or her perspective on change.

You should give four things to the main person. The first is vision. The main person must understand your vision and commitment as well as the sacrifice you will make for the change. Second, you must give the main person ownership for the change. John believes that the leader must give main persons a piece of the pie. Until they have had input into change, they will not buy into the new project.

Third, the main person must have your support—and vice versa. Maxwell says the greatest resource you can give to the main person is your support. And the fourth thing to give the main person is time. Since you want to change things in his or her area of responsibility, set up a series of meetings in order to develop understanding. Then the two of you can move forward together.

John warns that if main persons are bypassed they will torpedo the agent of change. But if you work with them properly they will say, "This change is our idea."

Circle 3: Decision Makers

When you enter this circle, Maxwell says, you are among the movers. Here you are not looking for input, but for influence. These people are more than position holders; they are decision makers. Maxwell tells his staff that this is the most crucial circle a leader can enter.

The movers are the members of the board, the deacons, the finance committee or the music committee. If a majority of the decision makers are positive toward change, bring all of them together for a discussion. Those who are positive about the change will take care of the battles with others. If the negative group is larger, meet with them individually. Ask for feedback without decision. "In other words," Maxwell says, "when you've got it going *for* you, bring them together. When you've got it going *against* you, deal with them separately. Don't let them get together to kill change."

Maxwell says the pastor should know what "turns the crank" of each board member. You should know how to get these members on your side, see your vision and feel your burden. When asked about knowing what turns the crank of the board members at Skyline, John says, "That's my job."

He illustrates the point by recalling an experience at his previous church in Lancaster, Ohio. Before Maxwell became its pastor, he attended a church business meeting and watched members go through a battle over whether or not to build an activities building. One-third of the congregation said if the activities building were constructed, they would walk out, and the remaining two-thirds said if it wasn't built, they would get mad.

When Maxwell became pastor he realized he was going to have to handle the issue of the activities building carefully. Basically, he didn't want the activities building because it was to be built where he wanted to build the sanctuary, and because he had other plans for the church. Soon after arriving, he instituted a committee to investigate every possibility. It took them 10 months. One year later the church had grown so rapidly that everyone realized they needed a larger sanctuary, not an activities building. When they took a vote, only one person in the entire church voted for the activities building. Everyone else voted for the new sanctuary. Why? Because the burden was now soul-winning, not recreation.

Later, Maxwell was faced with the need for an activities building. He wanted to use the old sanctuary, but he knew that would never fly because many of the people had been saved at the altar in the old sanctuary and they would not want it used for basketball. Maxwell brought all the decision makers (board members) together and said, "Let's not vote on it, but let's talk about how we can use the old sanctuary. In a brainstorming session, a new Christian who had not gone through old battles spoke up: "Let's make it into a gymnasium." The old members were not threatened because they were not voting on the idea. After a long period of discussion the tide turned because the need was evident.

When the "main person" finally became convinced that they needed a gym, John knew the change would be successful because the main person had been the leader of the opposition. He told Maxwell, "If you're ready to make the sanctuary an activities building, I am ready to support you."

Circle 4: Those Most Affected

Who will be affected most by the change? For example, changing the Sunday School program affects teachers and other workers most directly. When you enter this circle Maxwell says you are looking for involvement. Do three things:

1. ask for input;
2. appeal to their interests and;
3. allow them concessions for their needs whenever possible.
John says when he goes into meetings with workers in the fourth circle, he plans to make concessions. Why? Because they need to see that they have input and influence.

Circle 5: The Members

This circle involves the people or the church members. When John Maxwell enters this circle he is looking for their intention. The question is: Will they follow the leader? This is the easiest of all the circles to get an affirmative vote for change. If the first four circles are positive, the people in this circle will say yes. Most large churches have easy business meetings. Why? Because the pastors are effective leaders and carry out the process properly.

Throughout this entire process, two factors are crucial: *timing* and *courage*. Maxwell understands the necessity of timing in making changes. He knows that people resist something they don't expect. "Resistance is always greatest when change comes as a surprise," he says. His experience has led him to these rules:

The Maxwell Rule of Timing

- The wrong decision at the wrong time is a *disaster.*
- The wrong decision at the right time is a *mistake.*
- The right decision at the wrong time is *unacceptable.*
- The right decision at the right time leads to *success.*

As for courage, Maxwell simply says if you know what you are doing, and plan properly, "Go for it." He remembers going to a church that had only 30 members. As John talked to the members at the board meeting, he found them pessimistic. They had had 30 people for 30 years. He laid out some things they needed to do to change. One of the five board members raised his hand and said, "We can't do that. If we made all those changes we might fail."

John laughed and asked, "What have you been doing—succeeding?"

This church held on to the past and was afraid to take any risks. Unfortunately, a majority of its leaders were among the 16 percent that Howard Hendricks says usually hinder a church's ministry. Many pastors become disheartened because they allow 16 percent of the people to ruin the church and their ministry. Instead, we should focus with courage on the 84 percent who are willing to do great things for God.

2

INNOVATIVE STRATEGY FOR MINISTRY

Willow Creek Community Church
South Barrington, Illinois

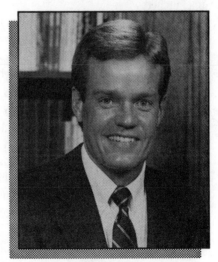

Rev. Bill Hybels, Pastor

THE SECOND-LARGEST CHURCH IN AMERICA HAS A WEEKLY ATTENDANCE of over 14,000. Willow Creek Community Church is also one of the most innovative churches in America because of its creative programming and, more importantly, because of its unique philosophy of ministry and its well-thought-out strategy for reaching the unchurched.

The $15 million facility is located on 120 acres in South Barrington, Illinois, 30 miles from downtown Chicago, and looks more like a civic center than a church. The grounds are more like a landscaped park than a church campus. None of this is an accident. Everything at Willow Creek, from the physical surroundings to the scheduling of services to the selection of music, is designed to create a comfortable, nonthreatening environment for the unchurched.

The weekend services—one on Saturday night, two on Sunday morning—feature drama, multimedia presentations and a 25-piece instrumental section backing quality vocalists who offer the best in contemporary Christian music. Bill Hybels, 38, the founder and senior pastor of the church, describes the weekend services as "seeker services," designed specifically for the unchurched. The audience doesn't sing hymns or repeat the Lord's Prayer, because, as Hybels says, "People who don't yet have a personal relationship with Jesus Christ can't honestly sing, 'O How I Love Jesus' or address God as 'Our Father who art in heaven.'"

People attending Willow Creek do not sit in pews, but in 4,650 individual theater seats. Nor do they see a robed choir or listen to organ music. Hybels, in a business suit, looks less like a clergyman than an executive commuting to the Chicago loop. Although his message content is biblical, and he is committed to the inerrancy of Scripture, his speaking style is more that of a marketing specialist than a preacher.

Hybels uses a plexiglass lectern rather than a pulpit and majors on communicating, not on traditional liturgical preaching. He believes the Bible is totally relevant to twentieth-century man and ought then to be communicated in a relevant, practical way. While he teaches expositorally from the Scriptures at his mid-week services, designed for believers, at the seeker services he presents a biblical perspective on topics that might be raised on a television talk show by a Phil Donahue or an Oprah Winfrey. Hybels' aim is to make the Word of God "user-friendly" for contemporary Americans.

An Innovative Beginning

Hybels began the church in 1975, while a student at Trinity College in nearby Deerfield, Illinois. The church's name came from the Willow Creek Movie Theatre, which he rented for his Sunday services. Frustrated with the traditional church and with, what he perceived to be, dead ritual and meaningless liturgy, and aware of plummeting attendance in most mainline churches, Hybels decided to try a new approach to reach disenchanted Baby Boomers like himself.

Before starting the church, Hybels and several friends spent four weeks doing a door-to-door survey. They asked, "Do you regularly attend a local church?" If the response was no, they asked, "Why not?"

They learned there were four primary reasons people didn't go to church:

First, people felt churches were always asking for money. Hybels decided then and there to adopt a low-key approach to money. During the first few years of the church, he collected no offering; attenders placed their contribution in a basket in the back of the theater. Eventually overcrowding made that logistically impossible, and now a collection is taken.

But visitors are still informed each week that they aren't

expected to contribute: "You're our guests. Just sit back and enjoy the music." Regular attenders are challenged to tithe, but there are no pledge cards, envelopes or high-pressure tactics.

Second, people said the sermons were boring and the services routine. One man told Hybels, "I don't have to go to church. I went for 15 years and figured out the whole system. I know just what's going to happen."

Hybels expected this complaint from "the media generation," accustomed as it is to fast-paced, creative communication. So he vowed to experiment with communication forms not usually associated with church.

Third, people believed church was irrelevant to real life. One man said straight out, "Church has nothing to say to me. The Bible is out of date."

After hearing that complaint over and over again, Hybels told his wife, "So help me, Honey, I will *never* preach a sermon that does not touch everyday life. God's word is *relevant!*"

Fourth, people claimed pastors made them feel ignorant and guilty. After hearing this charge, the young pastor determined never to talk down to people or use guilt to motivate them to action.

Target Audience: "Unchurched Harry"

To understand Willow Creek Community Church, you have to understand its outreach strategy. Hybels, taking a page out of a marketing book, has determined a target audience and developed a general profile of the person Willow Creek can best reach. Called "Unchurched Harry," the typical target person is a 25- to 45-year-old professional male who is married, busy in the marketplace and disenchanted with the traditional church.

While many Unchurched Harrys have a distant Christian memory, that memory is becoming fainter all the time. Hence, Willow Creek's outreach ministry is in many ways cross-cultural. Just as an American missionary in China would have to adapt to the language, music and symbols of Chinese society, so must Willow Creek adapt to those cultural elements of its secular target audience—without, of course, changing or diluting the timeless, cross-cultural message of the gospel.

Defining the Target Audience

Hybels knows he can't reach all the thousands of people in his community, so he tries to be realistic. He limits his target audience to the largest demographic group in the area—middle- to upper-middle-class, white-collar families, focusing particularly on men.

Hybels calls Willow Creek "a safe place to visit...a safe place to hear a dangerous sermon!"

When asked about "Unchurched Mary," Hybels notes that traditionally the Church has been weakest in reaching men, and he adds that, "If you can reach the men, you will probably also reach their wives and children."

While some church leaders bristle at the thought of "targeting" a specific audience, John Maxwell, pastor of Skyline Wesleyan Church (see chapter 1), agrees with Hybels' approach. Maxwell says, "If a pastor thinks he can reach everyone, he is probably not reaching anyone."

Hybels believes that targeting Unchurched Harry should be the central thrust not only of a church but also for a pastor. He thinks many pastors are ineffective simply because they are trying to reach people with whom they have no natural affinity. He believes God uses individual pastors' unique gifts and passions to enable them to reach a specific group of people—the inner-city poor, urban fast-trackers, the working class, rural midwesterners, university students, suburbanites and so on.

"Generally," says Hybels, "a pastor can define his appropriate target audience by determining with whom he would like to spend a vacation or an afternoon of recreation."

Hybels described a frustrated pastor who heard about "targeting" and realized he was ineffective because he was a suburban pastor in a smokestack city. He confessed he didn't relate well to his people and didn't "fit in" with the social and recreational life of the community. Many similar stories have confirmed Hybels' belief that pastors are most effective when the demographic profile of their target audience is similar to their own.

Adapting the Services

Deciding to reach out actively to Unchurched Harry presented Hybels with a unique problem: How could he edify believers and evangelize unbelievers at the same time? He concluded that he couldn't, because the two groups had such diverse needs. So, for Unchurched Harry he designed the weekend seeker services, defined as "Christianity 101 or 201." As described earlier, these services feature contemporary Christian music, drama, media and basic biblical messages presented in terminology unchurched people can relate to.

Willow Creek believers attend the seeker services, too (often with a visiting Unchurched Harry), but for deeper spiritual growth they also attend the Wednesday and Thursday night believers' services (the auditorium is filled twice), defined as "Christianity 301 or 401." These services are devoted to expository teaching, corporate worship and prayer, congregational singing and a monthly observance of communion. While most churches have their "worship service" on Sunday, Willow Creek gathers for worship at midweek.

Seeker Services

Underlying the success of Willow Creek's seeker service is the firm

Willow Creek Community Church, South Barrington, Illinois

belief that unbelievers should never be unnecessarily offended. The message of the Bible may indeed offend them, as it points out their sin and error; but the method of presenting that message should be as inoffensive as possible.

A Safe Place to Visit

The author interviewed a former atheist who was converted at the Willow Creek church. He said he agreed to come to Willow Creek because there were no crosses or religious symbols. He said, "It was so informal and unpressured, I could investigate Christianity at my own pace."

The atheist seeker attended for over two years before accepting Christ. He calls Willow Creek "a safe place to visit." Hybels adds that it's "a safe place to hear a dangerous sermon!"

Because Willow Creek's Christians can trust the church not to offend their unsaved friends, they enthusiastically invite friends to come with them. One unbeliever leaving a weekend service said, "Church sure has changed since I used to go. It seems as if that service was designed just for me."

Hybels sees the seeker service as imperative in the work of evangelism. Willow Creek does not have a formal weeknight visitation program. Instead, church members are taught to build relationships with unchurched people, use the weekend services as evangelistic tools and then share the plan of salvation when the Holy Spirit provides an opportunity.

Hybels does not call people forward at services to receive Christ. Rather, he encourages them to talk with the person who brought them—or with a church leader if they came alone. He says most conversions occur in the parking lot after a weekend service or in local restaurants over Sunday brunch.

During the seeker service, visitors are not asked to identify themselves. Hybels learned early in his ministry that the typical Unchurched Harry wants one thing when he walks into a church: anonymity. He doesn't want to say anything, sign anything, sing anything or give anything. He wants the freedom to seek in solitude.

Hybels believes that most churches place unrealistic expectations on Unchurched Harry. They expect a person who has had a totally secular mindset for 20, 30, maybe 40 years to change his whole way of thinking for one hour on a Sunday morning. Willow Creek accepts the fact that for many people conversion is a slow process. Most Unchurched Harrys at Willow Creek attend services for six to eight months before accepting Christ.

Moving on from Conversion
Conversion is just the beginning of the Christian walk at Willow Creek. The next step is the midweek believers' service. Because of the pace of contemporary life, it's no small thing for a new Christian to commit one night every week to Bible study and worship. Yet, at every weekend service new believers are invited to the midweek service. What draws them most effectively, however, is the personal invitation of the person who led them to Christ.

At Willow Creek, the next step in a person's spiritual journey is involvement in a small group. These groups provide personal discipleship and accountability—a "small church" within the larger church.

Service is the next step, and Willow Creek's Network ministry helps people discover their spiritual gifts and directs them to appropriate opportunities for service. According to Hybels, converts who commit to the midweek service, submit to the challenge of a small group and devote themselves to service almost always move on to a final step: reaching out to other Unchurched Harrys and perpetuating the cycle of evangelism.

The Point Man Concept

Another of Willow Creek's foundational strategies is the "point man concept." Hybels says, "We learned never to start a ministry without a person who can 'walk point' and lead the new program effectively."

Finding God's Person

For years, Hybels says, Willow Creek postponed the development of a missions program because the elders could not identify the right person to embody the vision and make the sacrifices necessary to get a missions program started. The elders were often criticized as being antimissions, but they continued to wait for God to provide the right person. He finally did, and the missions program has since flourished.

In contrast, the church once responded to the large numbers of young singles in the community by starting a Singles' Ministry, in spite of the fact that there wasn't a strong leader. The ministry floundered for months and ultimately had to be shut down. Later, a godly couple with a passion for singles joined the church and developed a highly successful ministry. Although the need had been evident for some time, it couldn't be met effectively until God provided a point person.

That was a tough lesson to learn, but today Willow Creek endorses the concept wholeheartedly. The elders refuse to design or endorse any new program until the right person can be found to lead it. Hybels notes, "It takes enormous energy to prop up an ineffectively led program. Yet it takes very little energy to keep an effectively led program running. When you have the right person running point, the Spirit is free to sustain the ministry."

Qualifications of a Point Person

Hybels believes the point person must have two gifts. First, he or she must be able to communicate well with the unchurched. If ministry leaders aren't comfortable with unbelievers or don't have credibility with the unchurched, the ministry will never draw them. It will become an all-too-typical "holy huddle."

At the same time, the point person must be able to edify believers. One can't build an effective ministry unless he or she can move people into greater maturity in Christ. If a leader draws the unchurched, but fails to "grow them up," the result will be a ministry built on a weak foundation.

Effective Lay Involvement

Since one key to ministry growth is effective lay involvement, recruiting lay workers is serious business at Willow Creek. Says Hybels, "When it comes to recruitment, too many church leaders are 'slot' oriented. They identify a need in their ministry, then look for someone to fill that slot." To illustrate, Hybels describes a Sunday School superintendent trying to recruit a teacher for a fourth-grade class. "The typical approach," he says, "is to turn up the guilt thermostat and make an emotional appeal. If people feel enough heat, eventually they break down and 'do their duty.'"

But according to Hybels that approach often leads to disaster. If a person without teaching gifts ends up as a fourth-grade teacher, he or she will probably be ineffective and hate every minute of class—as will the fourth graders. As a result, that teacher will probably resign as quickly as possible and vow never to volunteer for service again.

Willow Creek has a different strategy for lay recruitment; it starts with people instead of positions. New members are challenged to discover their spiritual gifts so they can serve where they are most effective and fulfilled. Hybels uses the phrase, "every member a minister," to describe the goal of lay involvement. The church's Network Ministry offers seminars which lead members through a spiritual gift inventory workbook; then individual counselors help members determine their three strongest gifts and guide them into appropriate ministry positions. The result is a high level of lay involvement and a low level of turnover: when people are effective and fulfilled in their area of service—when they love what they do—they don't want to quit.

Strategic Staffing

According to Hybels, a changing attitude toward pastoral leadership is very evident among Baby Boomer churches. "In the age of specialization," he notes, "pastors are no longer seen as generalists. Like lay workers, they must know their gifts and serve accordingly. We don't hire a pastor to do five things. We hire him or her with a highly defined job description in mind."

Staff Qualifications

When adding a staff member, Willow Creek focuses on (1) spiritual giftedness; (2) specific call or passion (the ministry area that most excites the person) and (3) temperamental/relational "fit" with the existing staff. Hybels says that when people have the gifts and passion for a particular ministry and can work well on the ministry team, they will be naturally motivated for ministry. "All we'll have to do is coordinate their efforts."

Hybels calls this approach "strategic staffing." He claims that the important issue is not how many staff members a church hires, but how well suited they are to the jobs they're assigned. He also notes, "We hire staff not to do ministry, but to equip lay people to do ministry. If staff members can't equip others to serve, their ministries will be held in check by their own limited capacities."

The Pastor's Role
Hybels works with a three-person management team, to which all department heads report. Through the management team and department heads, Hybels' leadership fans out to all church employees. He sees his biggest challenge as communicating vision and values to his staff. He does this primarily through monthly staff meetings.

In addition, each fall the staff goes away for a week-long retreat. There Hybels offers staff members an in-depth look at the church's future plans and takes time to listen to their concerns. He believes that listening is a crucial part of leadership. "You can't be a good leader without being a good listener," he says.

Staff Relationships
Hybels also believes that when it comes to good leadership, the richness of relationships is as important as the greatness of the cause. Many of his key staff have been with him for 15 years. "If we weren't working together in this church," he says, "we'd be working together somewhere else. We've grown together, failed together, confessed our sins to one another, held each other accountable, and wept and rejoiced with one another. That goes a long way toward building love."

Hybels makes relationship-building a priority and strives to foster closeness on his staff. Each Tuesday approximately 250 ministry personnel have lunch together. Randomly arranged place cards guarantee a weekly mix of fellowship. An emphasis on team ministry forces workers out of isolation and into close, daily interaction with others. The church counseling staff offers periodic seminars on subjects such as conflict resolution and understanding different temperaments. As a result staff relationships provide a rich and fertile environment for personal growth and ministry effectiveness.

No Sunday Evening Service

Willow Creek has no regularly-scheduled Sunday evening service, not by default but by design. Hybels believes that most Christians need a spiritual "shot in the arm" more on Wednesday night or

If the church does not change, its future is bleak. But its future can be bright if it's willing to be Spirit-directed and not flesh-directed.

Thursday night than they do on Sunday night. He says, "If they have a great spiritual experience on Sunday morning, Sunday evening church seems a bit anti-climactic. But by midweek, they need another dose of spiritual encouragement." He compares any service added to the Sunday morning service to a "water break" for a marathon runner, and suggests that a runner is wiser to schedule his main water break halfway through the marathon rather than 100 yards from the starting gate.

This midweek schedule benefits speakers as well as listeners. Typically, Sunday evening sermons get less than a pastor's best effort because he's preoccupied with the morning message. Hybels feels he can present a higher-quality message if he can present it later in the week.

There are other practical reasons for not having a Sunday

evening service. Hybels points out that the motion picture and restaurant industries have their lowest attendance on Sunday nights, and says, "The church ought to pay attention to that and ask Why?"

He did, and concluded that most Boomers use Sunday evening to relax and get ready for the work week. On Monday they have to get up early to get their kids to day care or attend a business breakfast. Because that profile fits Willow Creek's target audience, Hybels decided to adapt the church schedule.

The fact that Willow Creek is a regional church makes that even more important. "It's unrealistic for us to expect our people to drive one hour each way to church twice in one day," he says. And he points out that having no Sunday evening service also frees the evening for small group meetings in homes and for special seminars and workshops.

Spreading the Vision

Although it has made no effort to duplicate itself through a satellite program or formalized church associations, Willow Creek is more than willing to serve and encourage like-minded churches and pastors. To that end, it holds pastors' conferences three times yearly. Each conference is limited to 500 people; waiting lists are common. Church leaders have come from Australia, South America and Europe to study Willow Creek's philosophy and to learn to implement its principles.

Hybels is enthusiastic about the conferences and encouraged by accounts of churches experiencing growth because of changes they've made. However, he recognizes that many pastors have failed in trying to adopt Willow Creek's methods. He believes this often happens because leaders copy Willow Creek's programs without changing their attitudes and overall church strategy. Hybels says, "Just starting a seeker service won't guarantee an influx of unsaved people into the church. The seeker service must be part of an overall philosophy of ministering to the unchurched. An upbeat band, a dramatic skit and a practical message are great. But they won't accomplish a thing unless Christians build credible relationships with the unchurched, invite them to church and talk to them about their faith. The seeker service must be accompanied by a transformed mind-set regarding evangelism."

Hybels acknowledges that it is extremely difficult to implement the total Willow Creek philosophy in a traditional church. However, he ends each pastors' conference by summarizing a number of "Transferable Concepts," and he firmly believes that many pastors could revitalize their churches by clarifying their vision and making workable modifications.

The Horizon

Bill Hybels says that, "If the church does not change, its future is bleak. But its future can be bright if it's willing to be Spirit-directed and not flesh-directed."

While Hybels clearly desires that Willow Creek be Spirit-directed and enjoy a bright future, he does not make numerical projections. In fact he says, "I see red flags when people talk campaigns, contests and numerical goals." He believes that emphasis should be on the causes that drive us, not on the numerical effects they produce.

He doesn't deny that numbers help evaluate certain aspects of ministry and make long-range budget/building projections possible. He even admits that "we graph on the basis of our latest growth trends, monitor and evaluate figures and let them give us direction." But he refuses to establish attendance goals. "Numbers should never be the basic motive for ministry."

Basic motive or not, numbers are an issue at Willow Creek. The three seeker services—Saturday at 6 P.M., Sunday at 9 and 11 A.M.—are approaching capacity, necessitating an additional Saturday evening service. Building a larger auditorium is not presently an option because the roads surrounding the church campus could not handle the traffic that would be generated by an expanded facility. Says Hybels, "We'll add multiple services as long as God continues to nudge people in our direction."

Hybels clearly wants to be a difference-maker. He claims he has never been motivated to pass on tradition. He declares, "Our mindset is this: If a program isn't accomplishing its objective, we need to let it die and mourn its passing—then get on with the business of trying something new."

3

A REFORMATION OF WORSHIP

The Church On The Way
Van Nuys, California

Dr. Jack Hayford, Jr., Pastor

"WE ARE IN THE SECOND STAGE OF THE REFORMATION," SAYS JACK Hayford, pastor of The Church On The Way in Van Nuys, California. This is not a reformation like the one led by Martin Luther, who got the Church's theology straightened out, but a reformation in which the Church is straightening out its worship.

The Lord is awakening His Church to worship, Hayford says. The original Reformation brought the Church back to the doctrine of justification by faith and the priesthood of the believer. These are foundation stones of Protestantism. But much of the spirit of the Church's pre-Reformation worship practices were retained, even though it changed its beliefs. Hayford sees coming a reformation in worship style that will transform the Church's outreach and growth. This change in one local church has come slowly, as Hayford has gone through his own pilgrimage.

The Church On The Way has grown dramatically in size and influence since Hayford became pastor in 1969. There were only a handful of members—18—meeting in a small wooden church building on a street called Sherman Way, in the Los Angeles suburb of Van Nuys. Originally called The Van Nuys Foursquare Church, the name was changed to The Church On The Way for several reasons. The new name identified the church's location at the busy Sherman Way address. It also identifies the church with Jesus, who called Himself "the Way," and with Christians who are willing to be "on the way with Jesus" to touch needy people (Acts 9:2; 19:23; 24:14).

From Promotional to Worshipful

When Hayford came to the church, he accepted it as a temporary assignment in addition to teaching at Life Bible College. He had been the national youth director for the Foursquare Church, and he admits that he was "promotion-oriented" at first. Now he says, "I have changed. I'm no longer dependent on promotion for the life of the church. People come to The Church On The Way because they are thinking people." He feels there should be no high pressure promotion, or tactics that use guilt, constraint or begging, to get people involved in the ministry. He says, "The Church On The Way is a happy place to be, but not a sensational place. Our growth has to do with biblical substance and Spirit-filled worship."

Worship Is for Nonbelievers, Too

The key to growth at The Church On The Way is the spirit of worship, not traditional evangelistic methods or outreach programs, Hayford says. "I originally thought worship was for believers, and evangelism was for the unsaved. God changed my thinking gradually to realize the Bible commands the unsaved to worship God: 'Make a joyful noise unto the Lord, all ye lands'" (Ps. 100:1, *KJV*).

Therefore when the unchurched enter a worship service Hayford says they focus on the interpretation of what we are doing so they may know, participate with and meet God. As a result, The Church On The Way has grown with little evangelistic preaching, a very untraditional altar call, no visitation program and rare evangelistic meetings. Preaching does not center on denouncing sin, but on exalting Christ.

This revolutionary approach to evangelism is working for Hayford and The Church On The Way because it focuses on new worship dynamics and experiences. Hayford explains it simply by saying that "a reformation in worship is in progress." He says it has been growing for a century, and is the hope of the future.

Refocusing Worship

Hayford is not talking about a return to the traditional worship service of the liturgical church. He makes a crucial distinction between what is done at The Church On The Way and traditional or formal services. The historic approach to the doctrine of worship has focused so much on God, in an effort to reunify His glory and underscore man's unworthiness, that an unwitting surrender to "works" in worship has resulted, he says. He sees many churches becoming "performance-oriented and hermetically sealed against simple love, warmth and emotion."

Worship is intended to introduce God's Kingdom power in the Church and extend that power through the Church.

As a remedy, Hayford says, the church must "redefine, unwrap and unseal" worship, returning to its original power and outreach. To him, "redefining" means that worship must be more than the adoration of God; it also includes intimacy between the worshiper and God.

"Unwrapping" worship means removing sectarian prejudices. For example, Jack feels that uplifted hands is no longer a sign of a "charismatic," but is a gesture to be used by all. "Unsealing" worship means that worship becomes a whole-person reformation process. Hayford is concerned about not only "worthily worshiping God because He deserves to be worshiped," but about what the worshiper gets out of the process. The worshiper is nurtured, healed and redirected by the process of worship.

Hayford says there is a "bite" in worship just as there is in sacrifice. Just as Old Testament sacrifice cost an animal its life, so our worship must include the offering of our lives. "As much as we want beauty, and as beautiful as worship may be, with God beauty is always secondary—life precedes loveliness." Even though

Hayford is Pentecostal and charismatic, he reacts negatively to some of what he calls "warm fuzzies" in worship, which are nothing more than feelings without substance or sacrifice.

Worship and Church Growth

Hayford believes churches will grow when three patterns of worship are pursued. First, Jesus must be worshiped because He shed His blood to redeem us from the curse of eternal death. Second, the worshiper has a priestly ministry that involves his duties and his purity. Third, worshipers are made a "royal priesthood," which involves kingdom authority.

Hayford says that, as priests, believers are also kings under the King of kings, and that God's presence in kingdom authority and power is the issue. He notes that worship is intended to introduce God's Kingdom power in the Church and extend that power through the Church.

Hayford's book, *Worship His Majesty*, is the best source for understanding what he means by the reformation of worship. There he explains that while "ruling" spiritually as a kingdom of priests is the privilege of believers, that rule is sustained by worship. Even to receive the command to be fruitful, multiply, replenish the earth, subdue it and exercise dominion is to realize that we must confess our dependency on a Creator so magnanimous that He shares His power with the creature. And to receive the command not to eat of the tree of the knowledge of good and evil is to perceive that we are so finite that we can only obey. Obedience, Hayford says, is the conclusive and ultimate response that true worship requires.

Worship at The Church On The Way

The worship at The Church On The Way seems to intensify when Jack Hayford steps to the platform. There's a spark that wasn't there before. Many have asked, "Why is worship more meaningful when Hayford leads than when others lead?" Jack Hayford is not just a worship leader; he's there to worship God, too. Basically, he worships God and invites others to join him in that experience. As a result, people experience what Jack Hayford is experiencing.

Hayford seeks to beget a spirit of expectancy in the church services. He studies more than his sermon. He plans carefully

---

The unsaved must feel the concern of the local body for their hurt and their loneliness.

---

what he does in a worship service and the way he does it. "I get my ideas in prayer on Saturday evening," he explains. When he begins worship on Sunday morning he always tries to get the people involved. He will say, "Turn to the person next to you and say, 'You'll love this worship service—it will be great.'" He hears the murmur of voices and sees the smiles.

Worship in Song

Hayford opens the worship service with a number of bright and assertive praise choruses that are upbeat and joyful. As a writer of hymns and praise choruses, he feels that mindless repetition of lyrics and melody is not worship. True worship requires the maturity of the mind as it interacts with the heart, which focuses attention on magnifying God. Thus, at some services Jack will begin, "This is one of those mornings when we must learn a new song."

After teaching the song he usually brings the congregation back to it later in the service to make sure they know it. He teaches a new chorus—often one he has written himself—about every three weeks, and will sing it two or three times until the congregation knows it well. He tells them with a laugh, "Let's not practice on God, let's practice on one another." So when the congregation sings the song, they sing it in worship to God.

As the worship progresses, Hayford moves toward the slower choruses of adoration, and hymns with more subjective expression. Hayford does not use hymnbooks in the worship service, observing that they make people stare at their laps. Rather, an overhead projector is used to project the words so people will look up as they sing. He always includes a hymn of the morning, one of the old hymns of the faith. He wants to keep a sense of history in worship. His wife usually leads this hymn, which is printed in the bulletin (since it is in public domain and involves no copyright problem).

The Church On The Way does not use a traditional choir to lead in worship, although a choir is a part of the church's life. When asked why, Hayford replied, "First, we are not a platform-oriented church. We are people-oriented, and the Bible commands, 'Sing unto yourselves.' So we do not have the choir sing to us or do our worshiping for us." Hayford believes the choir is often allowed to become a substitute for the congregation's worship.

Even though there is no choir on the average Sunday, a choir is sometimes used to teach new choruses to sing during the communion service and on other special occasions. There is no choir loft, however, they sing from risers. But even then, Hayford says, "The choir is not used for its performance or entertainment ability, but rather to lead people in worship."

Prayer and Ministry Time

The morning worship also includes what Hayford calls "ministry time." At this stage, attention is focused on the interaction of the body, with people praying in small groups. Ministry time takes about 12 to 15 minutes, with some four to five minutes spent in actual prayer. Hayford says, "Ministry time allows the Holy Spirit to minister through the church body to each individual."

The audience is asked to form small circles for prayer. Jack notes that getting people involved in small groups seems to paralyze resistance in those who are unsaved. He says with a smile, "The unchurched like this part of the service, realizing the personal nature of the time. They respond. But often, church people who visit our services will have problems with this aspect of our worship." When Hayford is criticized for dividing the congregation into prayer cells on Sunday morning he responds, "It's peculiar to expect people to come to church and not pray together."

Hayford points out the natural progress of the worship service. Singing choruses and hymns communicates the presence of God to everyone. This is the first step toward evangelizing the lost. They must feel the presence of God as they enter the house of God. The second step naturally follows. The prayer circles communicate the love of Christians to the unsaved. They are touched as someone holds their hand or hugs them after prayer is over. "The unsaved must feel the concern of the local body for their hurt and their loneliness," Hayford observes.

In small groups people melt under the care and love of other people. Hayford sees some people crying, others worshiping and some just enjoying the presence of God. He believes that there are more resolutions to problems and more healing in these small groups than at any other time in the life of the church.

To facilitate this small group prayer time, Hayford often walks to the center of the room. He wants to break up the congregation's fixation on the platform. He wants them to realize that this is not a "pulpit-driven church" but a "people-driven church." In essence, his standing in the middle of the sanctuary creates a big circle. Everyone stands and faces him. Then he announces, "Let's make small circles." He notes that "God never intended the church's ministry to be confined to a platform."

As the people stand in small circles facing him, Hayford announces, "We not only call upon the Lord, we expect Him to do something in your life. We want you to know His love and power to you and through you." He encourages everyone to share prayer

**The Church On The Way, East Campus Sanctuary (Main Campus)
Van Nuys, California**

requests concerning the problems, hurts or desires of each person. "If you have no request to share, we understand," he assures the congregation.

Before Hayford asks the people to begin praying, he quotes prayer promises from the Word of God, then exhorts the congregation to put into practice what they just learned. He asks the people to reach out to those in front, beside or behind them, then announces, "Make sure no one is left out of a group."

Because some people are frightened about praying in public, Jack assures them, "You can just join in silently, but if you do, join in with your heart." He encourages the people to hold hands while praying, and to sensitively embrace each other afterward, showing their mutual support. "The physical touch affirms that support," he says.

Organ music forms a soft background to the prayers. "Sound in the room helps eliminate self-consciousness when people are praying," Hayford says. To close the time of prayer, he begins singing softly. Others join in as they finish praying until all are finished and singing. Jack concludes the prayer time: "While you hug one another say, 'I believe the Lord heard our prayers.'"

Preaching and Teaching Time

Hayford calls the third part of the worship service "teaching time." He says if you have something to say, people will listen to you. In content and style, Jack's presentation is more like teaching than traditional preaching.

"I'm self-disclosing in my teaching ministry," he confesses. He feels it is mandatory to reveal his own struggles, because when the audience hears his story they identify with him. He realizes that some ministers are uncomfortable confessing their struggles before the congregation. To this Hayford answers, "You never lose your authority by being human as long as it's clear that your pursuit of God is holy."

Hayford stopped using the traditional evangelistic invitation years ago. "I realized how much I was depending on inducing guilt," he says. He feels that the repeated singing of an invitation hymn, with repeated requests to "come forward," probably does more harm than we realize. People already know their failures—"They know that 'all have sinned,'" he says. "I don't seek to focus guilt on them, but rather to point to relief from guilt by explaining how they can come to Christ." The unsaved recognize the relevance of the message and are told what to do. First, they sense the presence of God in the singing of worship choruses. Second, they sense the love of other people for them in the prayer circles. And third, they learn in the teaching portion of the service what they need to do to get right with God.

A Christ-Centered Conclusion

"Before we conclude," Hayford will say, "I realize some of you have never asked Jesus Christ into your life. If you haven't invited Him into your life, you are like I was at one time. I needed a Savior, and there is only one—Jesus, the Son of God. He said that He is God's Son, and that He would die for your sins. He did die, but He rose again to prove His word."

Hayford concludes by instructing them, "We will pray, and I want you to agree with Jesus Christ that He is the Son of God and that He has died for your sins."

After Hayford has prayed for the people he announces, "If you just confessed Jesus Christ, lift your head, look this way and signal with your hand so I can see you." He wants new Christians to do this after they are saved. He believes that lifting the hand or walking an aisle is hard to do before people are saved, but easier after they have made a faith commitment to God. Also, public confession is not confused with salvation, but is something the person does to strengthen his new faith in Christ. "Tell the person next to you, 'I am receiving Jesus Christ,'" Hayford encourages the convert. In this act he does not create guilt but rather helps the convert experience acceptance by people around them.

"This is a holy moment," he says to the audience. "First, let's thank God for those who were just saved." Hayford does not give an invitation to come forward and pray at the altar; nor are new converts introduced to the church. Instead, Hayford says to the new converts, "All who have acknowledged receiving Jesus can go to the next room to receive a packet of information to help you live for Him. The pastoral staff will be there to meet with you." He points to a sign over the exit that reads, "New Life Room," and says, "We are not receiving members into the church. We are there to help you get started in your Christian life and to pray with you."

Next, an offering is taken. During this time the announcements are often presented by video over television monitors in the sanctuary. In many churches, the announcements are long and drawn out, even tedious. At The Church On The Way, the video announcements are done vividly, cleverly and briefly—just the way the people hear announcements over television.

There is no benediction. Hayford dismisses the congregation by saying, "Don't take three steps without saying to a friend...."

One Church, Two Locations

Jack Hayford has focused on reaching the Baby Boomers of the San Fernando Valley. Whereas 20 years ago busing was a great evangelistic tool to reach children for Sunday School, The Church On The Way has focused on reaching young couples. At the present time the Sunday School is booming because these parents bring their children to Sunday School and remain to worship. But, like most growing Sunday Schools, the church has the usual problems of space, staffing and recruiting volunteer workers. The space problem has been solved by acquiring an additional location. The congregation's response to the challenge to serve has been positive, and the church is excited about outreach.

Although there were only 18 members of the Foursquare Church when Hayford came, they met in an auditorium that seated over 200. In their traditional Pentecostal style, they called each other "brother" and "sister." Sensing that the people didn't really feel the meaning intended in such "brotherly" terms, Hayford announced, "I am going to call you by your name." He wanted them to feel like family, and to know each other. Apparently this goal was reached, since he has lost none of his original flock— they have all followed him in his pilgrimage of worship. Along with the influx of new members, the problem of remaining "family" to each other has become crucial.

About two weeks after Hayford came to the church he was driving down Sherman Way and was detained about 30 seconds at a stop light. He was stopped near the First Baptist Church, and he realized that his face, on the side nearest the Baptist Church, was hot. He had sublimated his feelings about that church, which at the time had one of the largest Sunday Schools in America. Hayford had to confess, "Lord, I know what I feel toward that church

**The Church On The Way
West Campus Sanctuary
(Former First
Baptist Church)
Van Nuys, California**

is not right." He turned to face the church building directly—and the heat began to go away from his face.

That morning in his car, Hayford was convinced that the Lord was saying to him, "I am calling you to pray for that ministry." He began to pray for First Baptist Church in Van Nuys, especially that its leadership could keep up with the magnitude of its ministry. As Hayford drove away from the stop light he began to get peace, and to realize that even though he was ministering totally in their shadow, God would give him a ministry, too, even though a different one. Since his heart was now right, God could bless Hayford's own ministry.

This incident was predictive of a future relationship that Jack Hayford would have with the First Baptist Church. When the incident occurred, Van Nuys was an upper-middle class community. Located not more than 10 miles from Hollywood, it was home for many entertainers from the movie industry. Over the years, the neighborhood has become home for a variety of ethnic groups, bringing with them an entirely new set of social problems. First Baptist Church planned to move west with its people, and its facilities were put up for sale.

The Church On The Way considered moving, but God wouldn't direct Jack Hayford to do it. He said, "I believe that our call is to serve the city, and we're seeking every means we can to use every talent in our congregation to be ministry-oriented to the city." Over the years they have purchased stores and apartment buildings, expanding slice by slice of property at a time. They even bought out a liquor store to use the building for ministry. "I believe in mobilizing the people of God to give themselves to the city," Hayford says, "not with a handful of tracts but with the power of the Holy Spirit as they reach out to serve people and love them."

Then one day Dr. Jess Moody, pastor of First Baptist Church, came to see Jack Hayford. He offered to sell the Baptists' facility to The Church On The Way. Even though it was about a quarter of a mile away, the property met several needs, and the decision was made to purchase it. The price was $11 million. An additional $4 million in renovation will bring the expansion up to a price tag of $15 million.

The Foursquare auditorium seats 2,400, and the auditorium at First Baptist seats 1,600. The congregation will use both auditoriums as alternate locations to solve the problem of parking between services. In addition to the additional auditorium and parking space, The Church On The Way has gained facilities for all the choirs, and for a Christian school—a total of 125,000 square feet of building space, on 10 acres.

The expanded geographical parish church is an idea we will hear more about in the future. In this case, the close proximity of the two campuses means that The Church On The Way only partially fits this model. But its move in this direction is another indication of how this dynamic congregation is continuously open to innovation, and to truly being The Church On The Way.

4

THE MOST EFFECTIVE CELL MINISTRY IN AMERICA

**New Hope Community Church
Portland, Oregon**

Rev. Dale Galloway, Pastor

PERHAPS THE CHURCH WITH THE MOST EFFECTIVE SMALL GROUP MINistry in America is New Hope Community Church, Portland, Oregon. The healing that God did in the life of Pastor Dale Galloway before he began the church is the type of ministry that is evident in the approximately 500 groups that make up the life of the church today.

Possessed by a Call and a Dream

Galloway never forgot the vivid call to the ministry he received from God at age 15. Empowered by that call, he graduated from a Christian college and seminary, then pastored three churches before his life fell apart in 1970. His wife of 12 years divorced him. And when her plane took off for the distant Midwest, all of Dale Galloway's dreams for pastoring a church left with her.

Can a divorced man remain as pastor of an evangelical church? Years ago the answer was no. But Galloway was living in the Pacific Northwest, an area he calls the most unchurched section of America. This region was also secular America with a 50 percent divorce rate; and many here were willing to forgive him—especially if he could help them.

Because Galloway knew God had called him, he wouldn't give up. He also knew instinctively that God wanted him to plant a church. Even with all the odds against him, he would eventually do just that—he would plant a church. It would be a church unrestrained by denominational biases or self-imposed ecclesiastical boundaries. It would be a church with new hope for broken people, so Galloway determined to call it New Hope Community Church.

Then Margi Watson, herself a pastor's daughter, came into Galloway's life. They were married two years after his divorce and together they began a new life. Margi proved to be just as committed as he to his vision of planting that new church.

Galloway made his commitment to Christ to begin New Hope church while attending a conference at Robert Schuller's Crystal Cathedral in Anaheim, California. He remembers praying in the chapel on the top floor of the Crystal Cathedral's Tower of Hope with an attitude of "possibility thinking"—a Schuller slogan. There Dale had a vision of building a church with a congregation of 1,000 people by the tenth year.

But needing money to start the church, Dale and Margi put their house up for sale and moved into an apartment, using their $6,000 equity to begin the new church.

Preaching in the Rain

New Hope Community Church began in October 1972, with Margi leading the singing and Dale preaching from the roof of a snack shack at a drive-in theater on 82nd Avenue in Portland. About 50 people listened to his message that first Sunday over their car speaker phones.

Galloway had been inspired by Schuller's successful ministry, which also began at a drive-in theater. But looking back on this idea, Galloway notes that Schuller was in southern California where, for much of the year, it never rains. Now he says, "It was crazy to begin in a drive-in theater in Oregon, because it rains so much in the Pacific Northwest. Most of my sermons were preached in a raincoat." He indicated he wouldn't do it that way again.

Galloway's strategy was three-fold:

- to have a positive, uplifting service on Sunday morning,
- to involve everyone in ministry so people could minister to people, and
- to have home cell groups to network people to one another in the body.

Dale Galloway had a vision of the need and effectiveness of small groups before he began New Hope. Although Rev. Paul Y. Cho, pastor of the large Full Gospel Church in Seoul, Korea, is the pioneer of small groups, Galloway didn't get his idea from Cho. It wasn't until 1978 that Galloway finally visited Seoul, to study the small-group movement there with approximately 170,000 in attendance at the time. Galloway returned to the United States and

---

The threefold purpose of TLC (Tender Loving Care) groups is discipling, evangelizing and shepherding.

---

used what he learned to improve his own small groups. Today he is a member of the board of directors of Cho's International Church Growth Organization and also speaks at Cho's pastor's conferences.

Growth at New Hope Community Church didn't come easily. During the first eight years, the church met at 12 different locations. However, God honored Galloway's vision and a few months prior to its tenth anniversary, the church took in its thousandth church member.

At the tenth anniversary, the church was not meeting in a drive-in theater, but in its own building. By 1990, New Hope had grown to more than 5,000 members. Its new goal is to reach 20,000 by the year 2000. By statistical measurements, this is a 28 percent growth per year over its 1990 membership.

Today, driving south on Interstate 205 and looking east, you will see an imposing 110-foot cross, towering over Clackamas Town Center, a major northwest shopping center that surrounds the church. New Hope has 14 acres along the freeway, plus 27 acres directly across the street on a golf course. Some 100,000 people live within 15 minutes of the site.

The church has built twice on this location, completing its present 115,000-square-foot facility in December 1986, at a cost of $10 million dollars. The 3,000-seat sanctuary is the largest in the Pacific Northwest. When this sanctuary is filled, Galloway plans to begin multiple services, as they did in the old building where, at one time, they met for three morning services each Sunday.

Find a Hurt and Heal It

But anyone can construct a large building. The question is: How are people attracted to fill the sanctuary, and what is the secret of keeping them bonded to the church? Dale Galloway's answer is the variety of ministries the church offers.

He describes each of the various cell ministries as a "point of entry" into the church. Church growth leaders call this strategy of reaching people through "side door evangelism." This involves "winning a hearing" first. Then, side door evangelism has a three-step approach. First, an attempt is made to win each unchurched person to a Christian; second, winning the unchurched to the church; and third, winning them to Jesus Christ.

Dr. Robert Schuller laid the foundation for New Hope's ministries, when he told Galloway, "Find a need and fill it, find a hurt and heal it." So seven days a week and 24 hours a day New Hope is committed to helping hurting people by ministering to their needs. New Life Victorious is a ministry for alcohol- or drug-dependent persons. Positive Singles is for those who are not married, the largest such ministry in the Pacific Northwest. Other ministries include the Blended Family Ministry, Separation Survival, Divorce Recovery, Counseling Ministry, Special Ed Ministry—plus additional ministries for mothers of preschoolers (MOPS), for victims of rape, for people with eating disorders and many other similar support groups.

"If you have a need, New Hope Community Church probably has a ministry to help you," an usher told me as I was leaving the church.

Cells Are the Church

Galloway was asked to describe how cell ministry works in his church. He responded, "Cells are not another ministry of our church, cells *are* the church." At present they have almost 485 cells, with 4,800 persons in weekly attendance at cell meetings. Galloway's vision, when he began the church in the early '70s, was to have one cell group for every 10 members; and today that ratio still holds true. They are called TLC Cells, the "TLC" standing for "Tender Loving Care."

The Purpose of TLC Groups

Technically, Galloway describes the threefold purpose of TLC groups as:

- First, discipling;
- Second, evangelizing; and
- Third, shepherding.

He explains that every group is given the goal of bringing a new family to Christ every six months. When speaking to his group leaders, he motivates them to go soul-winning, to reach people and to get them converted.

Galloway also teaches the lay pastors who lead the TLC cells to plan for one-hour meetings. He recommends that they greet everyone, sit where they have good eye contact with everyone present, and always leave one empty seat to tell the people, "We can grow." Don't leave too many empty seats, however, as these can discourage people.

New Hope Community Church, Portland, Oregon

In addition, Galloway channels requests for hospital visitation, prayer for the sick, absentee problems and any other problems to the lay pastors leading these TLC cells. They, in turn, make assignments to the people in their TLC group for outreach, nurture or encouragement.

TLC groups are not covenant groups, where people "covenant" to meet together for a certain length of time, such as 12 weeks, and then the group ceases to meet. According to Galloway, "Our Tender Loving Care groups are on-going, without closure."

Nor do the TLC groups serve as Bible study classes. Even though they study the Bible, the major focus is not on Bible learning, but on ministry to people.

At the same time, TLC groups are more than just "sharing" groups. Galloway believes groups that are *only* sharing groups exist for a while and then run out of steam. He feels his TLC groups, however, have a permanent flow because they are task oriented as well as need oriented.

The Activities of TLC Groups

Those who have never experienced a cell group in action usually think of it as a Sunday School class that meets in a home during the week. But nothing could be further from the truth.

The TLC groups at New Hope engage in three main activities:

First, they pray together. TLC groups begin with short, conversational prayer. Members share answers to prayer so they can track their progress in the Christian life.

Because everyone in the group prays, they are bonded together. This becomes a basis for outreach as well as ministry to one another.

Second, they study the Bible to apply it to their lives. Galloway points out, "It is never a formal study of the Bible, but a personal study of the Bible."

The lessons taught in the TLC groups, as well as the sermons preached by Galloway, are communicated in series. Galloway believes that people "learn best by saturation." As an illustration he spoke six weeks on stewardship, and the TLC groups spent the same time studying stewardship. He noted that giving rose dramatically as a result.

The same format was followed with prayer. He preached on prayer for six weeks and the TLC groups studied prayer for six weeks. Spiritual results also went up dramatically following this series.

When it comes to the actual lesson time, the lesson itself is not taught the way it is done in traditional adult Sunday School classes. Galloway writes the lesson, which has a strong bent toward the practical. The lay pastors who lead the groups are supplied with two pages of questions that help involve people in discussion and interaction on the lesson.

"A good TLC group is where everyone participates," observes Galloway. He explains, "If leaders do all the talking, learning goes down significantly."

Third, they share with one another—a testimony about what God has done, an answer to prayer or a confiding of a hurt in a life. In doing so, Galloway says, the people follow the admonition of James who said, 'Confess your faults...and pray for one another' (5:16, *KJV*).

After sharing, people pray for one another, encourage one another and actually help one another. Here the biblical mandate of the Body ministering to the Body takes place, Galloway says.

Finally, they fellowship together with something to eat.

One man at New Hope told me his TLC group was the highlight of the week. "The first thing we do is to get caught up on the news of the week in everyone's lives. We talk to one another, then we pray for one another. Then we discuss the lesson—everyone gets into it with their opinion. Finally, we order in pizza and keep on fellowshiping while we eat pizza and drink coffee. I wouldn't miss it for anything!"

A Choice of TLC Groups

"Americans like choices," Galloway notes, as the names of visitors are given to different lay pastors to invite them to various small groups. But both members and visitors attend whatever Tender Loving Care group they desire. This strategy is in contrast to Willow Creek Community Church in South Barrington, Illinois, where the church directs people to certain groups.

The Significance of TLC Groups

New Hope Church was awarded the 1978 *Guideposts* Magazine Church Award by Dr. Norman Vincent Peale, founder of the magazine and author of *The Power of Positive Thinking*. Peale cited the TLC program as the main reason for the award when he presented it to Galloway on October 26, 1987. Peale praised the program for providing spiritual and practical assistance to area residents. Mayor Clark of Portland read a proclamation declaring October 26 as "Tender Loving Care Day."

Growth by Conversion

In addition to its TLC groups, New Hope Community Church has a Sunday School that meets at the same time as both morning services. Along with a strong children's Sunday School, many adult electives are offered, some with ongoing classes. However, the Sunday School is only one part of the larger picture of reaching people and making disciples.

"We break out of the restricted box by multiplication of ministries every day of the week," Galloway explains. By this he means that TLC groups are meeting every night and throughout the city. He pointed to the building and said, "No matter what time you come to the church, you will find it busy with people in all kinds of groups." Wednesday is their big youth night, not Sunday evening.

"Hurting people bring other hurting people to the church, Galloway says. "Healthy people bring healthy people to the church." It's a principle of "like attracting like," he explains.

Because the church has been in the "healing ministry," a lot of hurting people are attracted to New Life Community Church. Galloway notes that they have 485 "points of entry" into the church through TLC groups, plus other avenues that are not TLC groups. What is the result?

The result is genuine growth. Yet the church has not grown by transfer growth, as approximately 80 percent of the people now at New Hope Community Church have never been in a church before. And members are probably too young for New Hope to have grown by biological growth. *It is a church built on conversion growth!*

Prior to beginning New Hope Community Church, Galloway was frustrated in getting other people to do evangelism. Early in his ministry, a leader in the Campus Crusade for Christ organization showed him how to be a personal soul-winner. For many years he tried to teach lay people how to do the same thing, but he feels that this effort was ineffective.

Galloway is now delighted in the fact that 90 percent of the lay pastors lead someone to Christ every six months. He explains that TLC groups and need-meeting ministries produce so many live prospects that it becomes a natural step in ministry for lay people to introduce others to Jesus Christ.

Lay Ministry Is Emphasized

Galloway emphasizes lay ministry at New Hope. Three levels of lay pastoring are involved:

- Level 1, lay pastor in training;
- Level 2, lay pastor; and
- Level 3, the lay pastor leader who supervises five other lay pastors with their groups.

About three times a year the church has a "Superbowl," a lay pastor training session. The Superbowl name was chosen to communicate excitement and to motivate people who are preparing to become lay pastors. Candidates meet on Thursday, Friday and Saturday for step-by-step training in every aspect of TLC groups.

After they complete "Superbowl," they are given the title "lay pastor in training." They are supervised for approximately 100 days. During that time they work in the ministry but are not given the final title of "lay pastor" until they prove themselves.

Ministry Structure

"In 1984, I reorganized the church to make sure that pastors and lay people alike were involved in the TLC groups," Galloway explains. Back then there were two levels of ministry: first the pastors and then the TLC leaders. Now, every pastor leads a TLC group ministry, which is really the vehicle through which most of his ministry is carried out. And since the cells comprise the church, the whole church is involved in ministry.

As part of the reorganization effort, Galloway divided his entire church into geographic districts. A district pastor was chosen for each district to oversee all the members, prospects, lay pastors and TLC groups in that district. As the church continued to grow and expand in its cell ministry, "specialty" districts, "created around particular needs or ministries," were added.

Presently, the church has seven specialty districts—New Life Victorious, Singles Ministry, Young Adult Ministry, Senior High Ministry, Children's Ministry, Junior High Ministry and Music Ministry. Each of these speciality districts has its own geographic pastor who is over the lay pastors and cell groups in that district.

Ministry Leadership

"The secret of our TLC groups is leadership," according to Galloway. "The groups are leadership-centered and multiplication-centered." By that, he means that district pastors are always looking for potential leadership to promote people into greater roles of ministry. "We reward those who develop leaders."

The church's emphasis on lay ministry and leadership explains Galloway's own description of his job: "My job is, first, to preach on Sundays, and, second, to make 500 lay pastors successful." To do this, he confesses, "I had to learn to let go of ministry and to motivate others for ministry."

At this writing, some 500 lay pastors direct TLC groups. Galloway says, "Our goal is to have 1,000 lay pastors by 1995, with 10,000 people attending our Tender Loving Care groups every week."

Ministry Methods

"We use the Southern Baptist method of infrastructure to produce growth in our church," Galloway says. "We line up our group leaders to work toward group goals, which means we build prospect lists, work our prospect lists and involve people in our TLC groups."

In addition to the large TLC network, New Hope has put into place a phone-calling system. "We call systematically all the members of our church every eight weeks," says Galloway. "We also call all the prospects every eight weeks.

"All this information is fed to our district pastors, who process the information and enlist their lay pastors in helping them care for the people. The phone ministry is to care for the people who

---

The successful church will be relational, need-oriented, relevant and aimed at helping people.

---

never get into the call system and who otherwise would fall through the cracks."

When new people come into the church, they are immediately involved in service. Galloway notes that members who have been inactive for a length of time are hard to motivate. "So we put new Christians immediately to work." When asked why he might use immature people, he states, "We do just like Jesus, who challenged people to take up their cross and follow Him."

Ministry Motivation
Motivation does not seem to be a problem in this church. Galloway relates this in part to a system of accountability. Spirit and desire grow out of accountability, he believes, and "Christians who want to be used of God, will be accountable."

Everyone, therefore, fills out a weekly report on their ministry. As a result, no one goes off on a tangent, no groups have split to form a new church and no group has left New Hope Community Church. "People are loyal to New Hope Community Church because they are accountable to New Hope Community Church," says Galloway.

If a person says he doesn't want to fill out a weekly report form, Galloway tells them, "Lay pastors fill out report sheets. If you want to be a lay pastor, fill out a report sheet." In the Friday pastoral staff meeting, the report sheets are discussed and analyzed. On an average week, the church makes 13,000 contacts with people in the Greater Portland area.

Ministry Model

Many people describe New Hope Community Church as an untraditional church. Dale Galloway responds, "To me it is not a matter of traditional ministries or nontraditional ministries. It is a matter of creating ministries that meet people at the point of their need and helping people to become disciples and to grow into producing disciples."

Galloway honestly believes his approach is the model for the church of the '90s. "The successful church will be relational, need-oriented, relevant and aimed at helping people."

New Hope's Theology

Wesleyan

Dale Galloway's roots are in Wesleyan theology. Reared a Nazarene, Galloway says, "John Wesley didn't emphasize 'event salvation,' nor did he press people into a decision through an altar call at the end of his sermons. Wesley's great approach to evangelism was relational." He points out that Wesley would offer his hand at the end of a sermon, and say, "If your heart is as my heart, take my hand."

Galloway knows that the strength of the evangelical revival through Wesley was in the small classes and society meetings, not primarily in preaching to the crowds. He observes, "In small groups people became accountable, more loyal to Christ and His church, and because of loyalty the revival rolled over the English countryside."

Biblical

Yet Galloway notes that "New Hope Community Church is truly a community church, in that we are theologically in the middle of Calvinism and Arminianism. We are more concerned with biblical theology than we are systematic theology.

"We do call people to the decision. We do this in public services in many different ways. We do this in all of our ministries.

"I never preach just a gospel message, but the gospel is woven in and out of every message. People get saved every Sunday in our church. I constantly call people to commitment to Jesus Christ, to 'sell out' to God. When we help people where they hurt, they want our Savior, who has motivated us to help them. If we aren't helping people, we are not a church."

Galloway is thankful for the good foundation that he received in his holiness background, but feels that it is important to go beyond the initial experience of being filled with the Spirit to learning to flow with the Spirit in ministry. For him, this flowing of the Spirit comes out of spending time in fellowship with the Spirit.

Relational

"The Holy Spirit works in a love relationship," he emphasizes, "a love relationship between husband and wife, between pastor and people, and between people in a TLC group." For Galloway, these relationships are more important to spiritual growth than programs. "I don't think a person can be filled with the Spirit when he argues with his wife, rebels in ministry or doesn't tithe."

Galloway goes on to say, "Holiness must teach people how to live. It's not legalism or empty profession."

Beyond the Horizon

For the future, Galloway sees New Hope filling up its 3,000-seat sanctuary multiple times beyond the present three Sunday services before having to build again. "No one knows how large a church can become in America," he says. "We want to continue to be one of those pacesetters, reaching beyond, where the hurting people are."

For the past seven years New Hope Community Church has grown at an average rate of 500 to 700 people a year. "I believe that in the years to come," says Pastor Galloway, "we can double that."

On the last Sunday in November 1989, I attended an evening service where the district pastors recognized lay pastor leaders and lay pastors. During that service I got a different vision of Dale Galloway. Galloway gave credit for the success of the church to district pastors, they gave credit to lay pastor leaders, who in turn praised lay pastors. And they passed praise on to the lay people for the strength of New Hope Community Church. There was no fleshly "buttering up" the pastor, no elevation of Dale Galloway as the charismatic leader.

Then I understood the strength of the church, and I began to understand Dale Galloway.

For a comprehensive study of the multifaceted ministry of Dale Galloway and New Hope Community Church, read Kathi Mills, *Broken Members, Mended Body: Building a Ministry with Love and Restoration* (Ventura, CA: Regal Books, 1988).

5

AN EXTENDED GEOGRAPHICAL PARISH CHURCH

Perimeter Church
Atlanta, Georgia

Rev. Randy Pope, Pastor

INASMUCH AS A CHURCH IS THE EXTENSION OF THE LENGTH AND shadow of its pastor, so the unusual geographical program of Perimeter Church to reach the entire metropolitan population of Atlanta is an extension of the unique vision of its pastor, Randy Pope.

Pope's original vision was to plant an innovative church that would have 100 different locations on the perimeter highway around Atlanta—it gets its name, Perimeter Church, from this vision. His burden was to reach the entire metropolitan area for Jesus Christ and influence its society. He knew he couldn't reach into every area of Atlanta so he prayed, "Lord give us the perimeter."

"I didn't want to build just one super church touching only one socioeconomic group in one part of Atlanta," he says. "Instead, I wanted to find a way to impact the whole of the city—reaching far beyond the influence of one church in one location." Hence Perimeter Church would be designed to be one "local church," but one that meets in many locations. It would have one senior pastor with individual pastors in each congregation, one board made up of three elders from each individual congregation and one program of outreach carried out by each congregation.

There are many unique features that qualify Perimeter Church as one of the innovative churches of America. The five focused on in this chapter are: (1) it is an extended geographical parish church; (2) it reflects a new strategy in pastoral leadership; (3) it has the characteristics of a Baby Boomer church; (4) it employs innovative scheduling; and (5) it reflects the emergence of a new kind of denominationalism.

The Beginning Vision

Randy Pope was the planting pastor of Perimeter Church, beginning his work in the summer of 1977. While a student at the University of Alabama, he was preparing to follow his father in the medical profession. During this time, however, he began to seriously consider the possibility of vocational ministry. He originally saw himself entering the parachurch ministry, never dreaming of starting a local church.

Nevertheless, he enrolled in the Reformed Presbyterian Seminary, in Jackson, Mississippi. While there, he had a conversation with missionary statesman John Haggai, who told him, "Attempt something so great for God that it is doomed to failure unless God be in it." This challenge became the motto for the Perimeter Church and the guiding principle of Pope's life.

When Pope finished seminary, the sponsoring denomination, The Presbyterian Church of America (PCA), was just getting off the ground, especially in church planting, and it was not starting churches without a core group. However, they wanted a foothold in Atlanta, Georgia, the beacon city of the South. Because Pope wanted to start a church where people had no presuppositions about traditional ministry, the infant denomination was willing to take a risk on the venture.

The Presbyterian Church of America paid Pope's moving expenses to northern Atlanta. The PCA planned to send him a monthly salary check, but he would not receive his first check for 30 days, so he arrived in northern Atlanta with less than $10 in his pocket. The young church planter did not have money to pay the deposit for the apartment, the first month's rent nor the deposit for the utilities, he and his wife Carol committed their financial need to God in prayer. They had heard stories of others stepping out on faith, with the needed money arriving at the last minute. Pope waited until 4 P.M. on Friday afternoon, expecting the money at any time; then he went down to the rental office to explain that he didn't have the rent.

"We can't receive money this late on Friday because we can't keep it in the office over the weekend," the apartment manager told him. Young Pope was instructed to bring the rent to the office on Monday morning.

That night they prayed, expecting money in the mailbox the next morning. But the mailbox was empty. In the middle of Saturday night, he got up to pray and received a sense that God would hear his plea.

The next morning Randy and Carol attended First Baptist Church in downtown Atlanta to hear Dr. Charles Stanley preach. They had seen the church on television and knew that Stanley was a great Bible expositor. Their hearts were hungry, and they wanted God to speak to them before they began a church.

They walked into the church foyer, and a friend met them as he was leaving the early service. They chatted in the foyer, and then the friend sat with them in the back of the auditorium, wanting to spend some time with Pope. This friend had sent him money while in seminary, but the seminarian had returned it.

As the young church planter sat in the First Baptist Church he knew he needed $600 to pay his rent, deposits and groceries until the end of the month. But he had told God his need, and he therefore decided not to talk to his friend about it.

When time came for the offering, the friend took out a blank check and filled it out. Pope expected him to place it in the offering plate. But as the plate came by, the friend tucked the check into Pope's shirt pocket. "I want you to use this as you have needs."

During the rest of the service Pope wanted to look at the check. He had not been told the amount. Only later when he looked at it did he realize that God answers exactly what is needed. The check was for $600. This was his confirmation that God would bless the church.

The Referral Method

Many people knew Randy Pope was coming to Atlanta, because as he talked with friends he would ask for names and addresses of their friends who lived in Atlanta. Pope calls this the "referral method" of beginning a church. He asked the believers who gave him names of prospects to write letters to those persons introducing Pope to them. That way, when Pope followed up with phone calls, asking for appointments, he invariably got in to see the people.

"I went to minister to people, not to ask for their help," Pope says. "I challenged them to be in Bible study." So he spent his first days contacting the names of friends of his friends, talking to them about his church and asking them if they were interested in Bible study. He began meeting with individuals, teaching them the Word of God. Some he met early in the morning for breakfast, others for lunch, still others in the evening. Some of these people became part of larger Bible studies.

The First Facility

At the end of July 1977, a group of 20 people met at the Radisson Inn at I-285 and Chamblee-Dunwoody Road for a Sunday evening church service. The new church was now under way. A five-man steering committee was organized to find a location for the church. They set September 13 as a faith-goal to find such a location. As the date grew nearer, Randy decided to act.

By this time, 50 to 60 people were meeting in Bible study groups. But it seemed that every place Randy looked for a location, the doors were shut. He told his wife he was going to see Cecil Day, the millionaire owner of the Days Inn chain of motels.

The way he got to see Cecil Day is another glimpse of the providence of God. An executive of Day's stature cannot be seen easily, especially by a novice pastor. Cecil Day is a philanthropist who has donated hundreds of thousands of dollars to Christian causes. Consequently, he is protected from do-gooders who are always asking for money.

When Randy Pope walked into the executive suite of the Day's Inn office building, the secretary was not at her desk. Pope walked over to Cecil Day's door, which was slightly ajar. As he began to look in, Day walked out and they startled each other. Quickly, Pope told him his vision of planting a church and indicated, "I want to rent a facility, I am not looking for a gift." Day explained that he had a busy schedule, but if Pope would wait for a while he would see him. After a couple of hours, Cecil Day gave him five minutes.

The Day Realty Company had recently moved out of a two-story building a short distance away on Buford Highway, in order to occupy a large, multistory modern building. The rental agent for Day Realty showed Randy Pope the empty building and told him the rent would be $4 per square foot—which amounted to $1,700 a month—plus utilities, which would be about $300, for a total of $2,000 a month. Pope didn't even have $200 a month, much less $2,000; it was all a step of faith.

Then the realty agent told Pope that Cecil Day wanted to give the new church a break in the rent. After he called Day, he told Pope, "Mr. Day must *really* want to give you a break." The rent was $50 a month, with no charge for the utilities. God had given them their first building, again an indication of His providence in the planting of this church. The first Sunday morning service was held at the new facility on September 25, 1977.

Expansion and Growth

Prayer meetings were held in homes, a prediction of future meetings in homes. There was also a DAWN (Discipleship And Weekly

Nurture) group for men that met early for training in leadership and discipleship.

The second congregation was begun west of the parent church in nearby Marietta, Georgia, in 1980. It began in a day-care center, approximately 10 miles from the parent congregation. A new con-

---

We are not well suited for traditional-thinking church people. We are too innovative. We are geared for the unchurched person.

---

gregation has been planted about every three years. Even when the parent church bought property in Gwinett County, some 20 miles east, only about half of the people moved into the new location, the others staying at the original site.

Today, Perimeter Church consists of four congregations. All have property, two have facilities, another has begun building and one is about to begin. In the summer of 1989, they were joined by an upper-middle-class black congregation in Decatur and a student congregation that had begun in Athens. This church was not in the original vision, because it is 90 miles from Atlanta. However, those who went to the University of Georgia shared the original vision of Randy Pope and began a perimeter-type church in the university town.

A Model for Mission

"We don't think so much in terms of model," Pope says. "We think in terms of mission." The model of an extended geographical parish is servant to the mission of reaching many people for Christ and impacting the secular culture. Pope went on to say, "We would not let our mission dictate our theology, but in everything else, mission dictates."

Compatible in Vision
Traditionally, the Presbyterian heritage has not allowed for the extended geographical parish church. However, the PCA has been supportive of what Perimeter Church has done and Pope is committed to the PCA. "While the model is not traditional, the vision is compatible with the PCA," Pope says. "We stay within the heritage of the Presbyterian Church, and we see our model as more biblical than any model in the contemporary church."

Progressive in Style
In the early days, approximately 50 people came from another Presbyterian church that was having difficulties. Pope met with the people and asked them not to come to Perimeter Church because it was progressive in style and they were traditional people. Although they came anyway, his concern proved true. Most of them returned to their former church.

Even today, Pope says, "We are not well suited for traditional-thinking church people. We are too innovative. We are geared for the unchurched person."

Adjustable in Organization
As Perimeter Church continued to plant new churches, Pope said, "I found each new church more difficult to start. I found myself putting off beginning a new church, thinking, I don't want more kids." About this time Carl George, director of the Charles E. Fuller Evangelistic Association, consulted with the church. His advice to them was that they could not fulfill their vision with several congregations in one church. As Pope began to rethink his model, he decided that the vision could not be completed with this model and that vision is more important than model.

Perimeter Church did decide to adjust the model. They decided on a new organization, but recommitted themselves to the original burden. They decided that all of the congregations would become "particularized"; that is, each congregation would become an organized church, separately constituted and indigenous (self-supporting, self-organizing and self-perpetuating).

Each church would give 5 percent of its budget to a new organization called Perimeter Ministries, Inc. (PMI). Pope is the CEO of the new organization but will not run it. "It will have a COO (Chief Operating Officer), and I will continue ministry at the parent church," he says. The main purpose of PMI will be church planting, citywide "mercy ministries" and church resourcing.

Pope was asked, "Isn't this starting a denomination?"

He replies, "The PCA is our basis of fellowship and we will stay there. PMI will be functional for the ministry of church planting and mercy outreach, but will not replace the functions provided by the PCA."

Presbyterian in Government

Under the former organization of one church and many congregations, Pope was asked, "Do you control the other pastors and the other congregations?" He answered that he did not dictate, but used his influence for direction and quality of ministry.

Pope explains, "All the pastors met once a week, and I moderated the meetings."

He adds, "I am the CEO, but I didn't dictate to them policy and ministry." Rather, they met together for correlation, total planning and major budget approval.

He says that he still influences the congregations by his values, not by programming. Not all of the churches follow the same weekly program.

Pope considers each pastor as a teaching elder or leader of leaders. Following the traditional Presbyterian model, the elders have the final responsibility for the church. Pope indicates, "We don't take programs to elders for their approval. We take "people situations" for them to handle. It is shared problem solving and shared leadership.

The ruling elders establish the policy of the church, the shepherd elders (pastors) pastor the congregation. Each one of the ruling elders has a sphere of ministry for which he is responsible for communicating information, ideas and solutions to problems. As an illustration, the elder in charge of the home fellowship groups will phone his leaders every month to see how they are doing.

Pastor-equipper Leadership

Pope considers his new model of pastoral leadership as one of the more innovative planks in the Perimeter platform. He explains that in the traditional church model, the pastor *does* ministry, and the lay people *receive* ministry.

In other churches a second model of pastoral leadership is used, in which the pastor and his staff recruit, train, deploy and evaluate all lay people in the ministry. The primary thrust of the pastor or the pastoral staff then is to assign lay people to serve in the church. The problem with this second model is that the staff cannot know the ministry to which God is calling each person.

Perimeter believes in a model in which God calls each person. The staff member is the equipper of ministry, not the assigner of ministry, and the senior pastor equips everyone in the church ministry. Pope refers to the staff as leader-equippers.

To explain the concept of the pastor-equipper model, Pope tells the illustration of a man who came into his church but who did not become active in ministry until he found out he had an incurable cancer. At the same time, another situation developed. A pastor from a church of like faith outside Atlanta phoned to ask Randy Pope to visit one of his parishioners who was coming to Emory University Medical Center for a special operation. Pope contacted his own member with the incurable cancer, asking him to make the pastoral call and to assume pastoral responsibility for the patient at Emory University Hospital.

"I don't know how to do that, Randy," the layman said.

"Then I've failed," Pope responded, "because I haven't equipped you. I will train you to make pastoral calls in the hospital."

Pope sees his role as equipping people for ministry, not as doing all the ministry himself. His aim is to use every person in the church in ministry.

After some training in this type of ministry, the lay person visited the patient, but he came back to Pope and said, "This man is not a believer, and is about to die. You'd better go to the hospital and witness to him before he dies."

Pope responded, "No, *you've* got to witness to him before he dies."

When the layman explained that he did not know how, Pope said again, "That's my fault. I haven't equipped you."

Immediately he taught the man how to share his faith and sent him back to the hospital. Thus, Pope sees his role as equipping people for ministry, not as doing all the ministry himself. His aim is to use every person in the church in ministry.

Taking the Trauma Out of Change

"Many fear change, so don't flag change," Randy Pope advises today.

"I used to sell change dramatically," he said. Then he explained how he previously challenged the congregation to

Perimeter Church, Atlanta, Georgia

accomplish dramatic things in innovative ways. "Five years ago I would have brought charts to my people and had a big meeting to explain why we were selling our location and moving the church to another piece of property."

But Pope found he was agitating "overconcern, simply because people have difficulty understanding change.

"So now I just explain why we do new things and how we do them. I tell people as little as possible about what is going to change, although I tell them what they need to know, and when they need to know it. I explain that the pastors have dealt with the issues, the elders have examined the issues, and this is what they need to know.

"I'd rather deal with the problem of lack of information, rather than the emotional response of people who get too much information and don't know how to deal with it. People are not so much concerned about church business as they are about good preaching, good teaching and how they fit into ministry."

He discovered early that even some who went through an Inquirer's Class for new members were opposed to change, simply because it is change. New persons attending these Inquirer's Classes are not required to join the church, but only invited to discover the nature of Perimeter Church and to access its offerings.

In these classes, Pope communicates his vision for the church. And, in sharing his vision, Pope not only explains the innovative structure and style of the church, but also prepares those in attendance for change. "Change is our friend, not our foe," he tells them.

He explains that while other churches change in theology and polity, the Perimeter Church is different in model and methods. "If new members come in expecting to change," Pope asserts, "they will not fight the model or the methods."

At the end of the class, the prospective members are challenged to do more than join the church; they are asked to become part of the ministry. Pope reports that 90 percent of those who go through the class join the church.

Worship Styles at Perimeter Church

Originally the worship services at Perimeter Church were very similar to a liturgical Presbyterian service with a doxology, hymns, choir and so on. Over the years, however, the style of worship has changed drastically. Worshipers no longer use hymnals, but sing praise choruses and learn music that is introduced by the overhead projector. Ensembles have replaced the sanctuary choir.

The sanctuary itself no longer has a chancel up front with communion table and pulpit. Instead, the platform is open and Pope stands before the congregation without a pulpit, just an open Bible in his hand. Musicians have changed from using a piano and organ to forming an orchestra, and services have added drama.

Pope indicates that one of the reasons for these changes is that he has become "unchurch" oriented. He says, "I used to think of traditional Christians and how to get them into the church. But now I try to remove the obstacles and eliminate the needless barriers that keep us from reaching the unchurched person."

He feels that the hymnal, the Doxology, the chancel and the choir are elements of worship for the Christian, but not for the unchurched. "People don't pay to hear a choir, but they go to concerts to hear solos and ensembles." He went on to say, "What fills their ears during the week is the way to reach them on Sundays."

Still, Pope has not eliminated the traditional heritage of the church. Once a month on Sunday evenings they have the traditional communion service for Christians. The hymnals are moved from the storage closet, the pulpit is brought to the front of the church and a traditional Presbyterian worship service is followed.

When asked about his preaching Pope said, "My style of preaching has remained casual." Someone made the observation that he does not preach "at" his congregation but talks "with" them. While this is called conversational preaching, Pope says he is simply a communicator.

He used to think the purest form of preaching was expositional, explaining a Bible passage verse-by-verse. But he has changed his opinion.

Now he has a balanced approach to preaching with an explanation of Scripture as it relates to issues and topics. "I want to begin with the needs that concern the unchurched person and take him to the Bible for answers," he says.

The church regularly puts on contemporary outreach shows designed to reach unchurched people. Recently Perimeter Church sold 3,000 tickets to a musical entitled "Back in Time." The people were taken back in time to analyze the music of the '60s—the music of the Baby Boomers. As they sang the secular songs that moved the Boomers in the '60s, the needs, hurts and motivations of the music were explained.

At the end of the show, Randy Pope talked about what people of the '60s were looking for, and how even today Christ is the ultimate answer. He explained, "I didn't give them a 'pray-a-long' prayer, but I told them how Christ relates to their needs."

After the show, people took their friends to a restaurant that had been reserved for dessert and conversation. Baby-sitting was not provided, because the pastor said, "This time is designed for our people to be evangelists. I don't want them to feel they have to run by the church to pick up their children, but rather that they have time to spend with the unchurched people." As a result, they sat in restaurants and talked to their friends about Jesus Christ. Over 200 came into the church because of this innovative approach to evangelism.

Summary

Randy Pope began an innovative church—an extended geographical parish ministry model—that followed a traditional worship model. But over the years continual changes have occurred. The traditional worship model has evolved into a creative form of worship. And the innovative idea of one church with 100 campus congregations has evolved back to a more traditional model of church connectionism.

The message has not changed, but the model continues to emerge.

6
NEW LIFE FOR A DOWNTOWN CHURCH

First Baptist Church
Jacksonville, Florida

Dr. Homer Lindsay, Jr. and Dr. Jerry Vines, Pastors

THE FIRST BAPTIST CHURCH IN DOWNTOWN JACKSONVILLE, FLORIDA, IS one of the largest, fastest growing and influential churches in the Southern Baptist Convention (SBC). In a decade when many churches in the downtown business area felt the sociological pressure to flee to the suburbs, the First Baptist Church has remained. It now owns nine square blocks in the heart of the city, and is perhaps the largest local property owner in a district where property is now selling for top dollar per square foot. The growth of skyscrapers in downtown Jacksonville's skyline places the church in a leadership paradigm for most areas of community life.

In one sense, the strength of First Baptist in Jacksonville is its traditionalism; but it is far removed from a traditional church. It is traditional only in the sense that it has not abandoned its conservative stance or its separatist posture; it is not traditional in its attitude and vision. It has an innovative strategy for pastoral ministry and innovative programs to attract singles, to teach men and to reach out to the lost in the metro area.

The church doesn't use "contemporary Christian Baby Boomer" music, yet it reaches Baby Boomers. It doesn't use innovative evangelistic methods, nor contemporary worship styles. Yet, First Baptist deserves to be listed with these churches that emphasize innovation and change, because of its ability to do the unexpected—that is, make a downtown ministry thrive while others abandon the same programs this church makes work.

One Congregation, Two Pastors

One of the most unique approaches to ministry is that First Baptist Church has two pastors who are coequal in every way. The two senior pastors, Dr. Homer Lindsay, Jr. and Dr. Jerry Vines, are equal in every aspect, yet their differing gifts perfectly complement one another. Their temperaments seem sovereignly preordained for this place and moment in history.

Pastor Lindsay said, "I had experienced being a co-pastor with my dad for four years, so it was not a new experience for me." He went on to say, "I felt that I could not properly minister in three preaching assignments every Sunday." Pastor Lindsay had recommended Jerry Vines, then pastor of Dauphine Way Baptist Church in Mobile, Alabama, to West Rome Baptist Church in Georgia. The two men were friends, and once when they were together Lindsay asked Vines to pray about becoming a senior pastor with him of First Baptist Church in Jacksonville. They met five times to talk, discuss and pray about the tremendous challenge before them.

"When he felt comfortable with the idea, I presented it to the deacons and they called him as pastor," Lindsay says. And he notes emphatically, "We are both pastors." They began by using the prefix to the title, but the "co-" was dropped after a short time. Now they are both called "pastor."

Vines feels First Baptist is the greatest challenge of his ministerial career. He notes of the two-pastor model, "As I study the New Testament there seems to be a plurality of pastors taught. I do not believe this is a command, but that it's an acceptable New Testament model."

Vines preaches at the 8 A.M. service, and has approximately 3,500 in attendance. Lindsay preaches at the 11 A.M. service and has about the same number. Vines preaches at the Sunday evening service, and Lindsay preaches at the Wednesday night service.

In 1983 Homer Lindsay, Jr. had a heart attack and was out of the pulpit for three months. Later he had open-heart surgery and was out for six months. Twice in seven years he was not able to pastor the church. He now says, "The Lord knew what He was doing by having two men pastor this church, because we never missed a step when I was not available."

Lindsay wonders why co-pastors are not used in more churches, even though he realizes that not just any two ministers could pastor a church together. He knows that "it takes two people with similar temperaments to work together."

Our church is an old-fashioned, soul-winning church. We are committed to going after people and winning them. This is our main program— this is all our program.

Vines observes, "In our situation here it has worked very well for myself and Dr. Lindsay to serve together as pastors. I would not necessarily recommend it as a model for others to follow. There has to be a unique combination of personalities of the pastors, maturity on the part of the congregation and understanding of what the role of the pastor is intended to be."

"I don't have any ego problem; nor was it difficult for me to establish him as an equal with me," Lindsay noted. He explained, "My dad did it for me, and I sought to do it for Dr. Vines." He noted, "We don't compete with each other, we complement each other." And with a twinkle in his eye he added, "The devil is our enemy, not each other."

The two men meet regularly to plan, pray and seek God's will for the church. Every Monday they meet with department heads. However, when Dr. Jerry Vines was president of the Southern Baptist Convention, Pastor Lindsay administered the staff. When Lindsay was out with a heart attack, Vines administered them.

Both men have identical job descriptions. Lindsay notes that "I didn't hire Dr. Vines. The church called him, just as they called me." He went on to explain, "I have never told Dr. Vines to do anything, nor how to do his job. The only thing I suggested is that he start a Thursday business luncheon, and that has been extremely successful." The church televises both of its Sunday morning services, and a recent rating was identical—both services had approximately 28,000 viewers each.

Old-Fashioned Soul-Winning

"Our church is an old-fashioned, soul-winning church," Pastor Lindsay says. "We are committed to going after people and winning them. This is our main program—this is all our program."

The church has approximately 1,500 people involved in a soul-winning visitation program every Wednesday evening. Lindsay said, "You know our people care for their friends because they go soul-winning." Vines adds, "Soul-winning is the reason why First Baptist exists."

To keep the church committed to soul-winning, one quarter of each Sunday School year is committed to teaching a curriculum that centers on soul-winning. The church wrote its own curriculum and the Sunday School Board of the Southern Baptist Convention is considering publishing it for other churches.

"We had tried to train our people in soul-winning by teaching them five consecutive nights," Lindsay explained. "This schedule worked in the '50s, but it doesn't work in the '80s or '90s. He also said that, "We've tried to teach soul-winning in the Baptist Training Union on Sunday afternoon, but only about 20 percent of our people attend on Sunday afternoon."

He concludes that "the most effective way to train our people to be soul-winners is to train them in Sunday School, because that's where most of our people attend." Even if a member attends only every other Sunday, "at least he's got some training in soul-winning," Lindsay said with a knowing smile.

First Baptist Church attempts to reach the entire metropolitan area of Jacksonville which—with its city-county government—used to advertise itself as the city with the largest geographical area in the United States. The evangelistic outreach begins with teenagers who do a survey of the entire city every year. In this survey, the church is looking for unchurched families that are not worshiping anywhere.

The teens go to the front door of a house and announce, "We're visiting for the First Baptist Church in downtown Jacksonville." The first question they ask is "Do you attend church?" If they get an affirmative answer, the teens thank them and go on their way.

If the people say they are not attending church, the teens attempt to get their name and address, along with the names and grade levels of their children. This information is fed into a computer, then given to Sunday School teachers. It is the job of the Sunday School to follow up on these prospects.

Each Sunday School class has two or more outreach leaders. Lindsay is often quoted as saying, "My most important meeting each week is with the outreach leaders." Prospects are assigned to the outreach leaders at Wednesday night visitation. Each outreach leader gets six prospects. When one of the prospects is converted and joins the church, then another prospect is assigned to the leader. Each outreach leader always has six prospects.

Outreach leaders do not go visiting by themselves, but with a visiting partner—which means the team has 12 prospects, six for each person. The church expects outreach leaders to contact each of their 12 prospects every three weeks by a home visit, a telephone call or a note in the mail.

Pastor Lindsay says, "We expect each prospect to get six visits from the church. On the first visit to the home, we tell our workers to give a witness to the Lord Jesus Christ. But even then, we try to cultivate their friendship and invite them to the Sunday School class."

The church uses the principle of "side-door evangelism" already noted in this book. This principle involves "winning a hearing" in a three-step strategy. Lindsay says.

- First, win the prospect to yourself;
- Second, win the prospect to your Sunday School class; and
- Third, win the prospect to Jesus Christ.

Lindsay noted that some people choose to go to church in their neighborhood rather than coming downtown. However, the growth of the church indicates the success of the program. After a person has been visited six times or asks the worker not to return, the name is dropped from the file and another prospect is given to the outreach leader.

Adult Sunday School

Reaching Men

Another innovation at the First Baptist Church is its men's department. In 1977, Pastor Lindsay divided the men and women into separate departments and began the men's department with 296 men. Today they have over 1,200 men in attendance, representing all ages.

Lindsay is the director of the men's department. He conducts an opening assembly each Sunday morning, makes announcements, provides motivation and is the driving force that makes the department successful. He says, "Men reaching men is the key to our church."

Vines is the cheerleader for the men's department. "The men's ministry is one of the most exciting ministries in our church," he says.

Each Sunday the men find seats in the 1,200-seat dining room. They arrange themselves around the tables by classes, drinking coffee and eating donuts. A 15-minute assembly features all the men singing and a devotional from one of the men.

Then they go to their classes. The largest class has 70 men, the average class has 35. This is a significant contrast to the typical Southern Baptist approach of 10 adults per class. The church has 28 men's classes.

Lindsay notes, "Gospel rock is a contradiction of Christianity. It's against all that is holy and spiritual. I am not going to use worldly means to reach lost people."

According to Pastor Lindsay, "You've got to have good men teachers—good leadership—before you can get a man involved in Bible study." He boasts that, "most of our men Sunday School teachers can preach as well as the average pastor of the average Southern Baptist church." He said the average teacher will study six or seven hours for each lesson because this is the greatest assignment in life. "I want excellent teachers to produce excellent men."

Reaching Women
The church follows the traditional SBC strategy with its women's department. The small classes of four to ten women are built around Bible discussion and fellowship. Lindsay noted, "The women like this approach, because they like to discuss the Word of God. But I have found that men don't want to be called on for discussion or to be put on the spot to answer questions."

To get accountability from Sunday School teachers, they are

required to be on soul-winning visitation every week. There is a teachers' meeting each Wednesday, where reports are received and strategy is shared with all teachers.

Lindsay noted that the church gets some objections to the division of adults into male and female Sunday School departments, but noted that "most of the objections come from the women, not the men." He did observe that some prospects think they won't like the division of men and women, but after the men come they like it.

Vines answers the objections: "It enables us to meet the needs of our men in a unique way. Through the men's department we are able to take advantage of the psychological differences and spiritual needs of the men."

Singles Ministry

The church advertises itself as having one of the largest singles ministries in the nation, with an average of over 850 in weekly attendance. Lindsay notes, "We were among the first to begin a single adult ministry." They have over 100 in the single parents class, choosing not to divide into smaller groups at the request of class members. The church has developed a 12-month curriculum on biblical single-parent helps.

Other Adult Ministries

The College Department has over 200 in attendance, primarily ages 18-24. The Career Department includes ages 25-35, with over 300 in attendance.

There is also a Newly Wed Class with approximately 80-100 in attendance. The church has developed a 12-month curriculum on marriage for those planning to get married.

Those who are getting married the second time attend the

Newly Wed II class, where their own unique problems and needs can be met. Again, they have almost 100 in that class.

Music: Baptist and Evangelistic

The church has a traditional Baptist approach to church music. With another twinkle in his eye, Pastor Lindsay said, "We changed the music when I became pastor. We got rid of Bach, Beethoven and anthems. We did away with the "Threefold Amen" at the end of hymns. We brought in evangelistic music, singing hymns and gospel songs."

Pastor Vines agrees completely: "I believe the music is to prepare the preacher to preach the Word and to prepare the people to receive it. I want our music to be evangelistic and done in the very best possible manner. Our music avoids the extremes of high church and rock/contemporary music. I want heart-warming, gospel music."

The church does not have a rock band as do many churches that appeal to the Boomers, although Boomers flock to the church. Lindsay notes, "We do not have electric guitars, drums or contemporary music."

He holds without apology that "gospel rock is a contradiction of Christianity. It's against all that is holy and spiritual." To further explain his position, he adds, "I am not going to use worldly means to reach lost people."

The church does not have contemporary drums, but does have kettle drums in an orchestra. In fact, there are four orchestras, each with approximately 50 members and sections that include violins, bass, winds and kettle drums. The Gospel Orchestra plays at 8 A.M. and the Chancel Orchestra at 11 A.M.

The church also has a junior high orchestra and a senior high orchestra. If a musician in an adult orchestra can't attend, one of the young people will fill in.

First Baptist Church, Jacksonville, Florida

History and Horizon

Homer Lindsay, Sr. became pastor of the First Baptist Church in 1940. His son, Homer Lindsay, Jr., one of the present pastors, was called as co-pastor on January 1, 1967. Four years later his father retired, at age 70. The senior Lindsay died in 1981.

Homer Lindsay, Jr. continued to build on the foundation laid by his father. Whereas the father led the church through his preaching abilities, the dominant spiritual gift of the son is his administrative skills, and he has directed the church toward a total commitment to evangelism and outreach.

In the early '70s the church had a strong busing program. Before coming to Jacksonville, the younger Lindsay also had a strong busing program in his church in Miami. "I have always been driven to reach people everywhere I have pastored."

He had learned in Miami that he could fill buses with children and thereby reach their parents for Jesus Christ. "The bus ministry was a tremendous blessing to our church because of the excitement it brought to the congregation," Lindsay said. However, church attendance plateaued for 10 years after it reached approximately 800 bus riders a week.

Enthusiasm for the buses died as the decade of the '70s drew to a close. The church dropped its bus ministry in 1978, when the program took a slump in attendance. This was the same time that they built the new sanctuary, and they found that new space provided a basis for reaching new people.

The church has always reached bus children, bringing them to the 11 A.M. Sunday School. However, with the new sanctuary and the excitement of the new building, they had difficulty attracting workers for the bus program—another factor in their dropping it.

Because they had outgrown the old building, they began planning for the new building that was occupied in 1978. There was great attachment to the old sanctuary, so Lindsay promised that the men's Sunday School department would meet there.

"We didn't build a new sanctuary to reach people," he says. "We built it to service the people we were reaching." But now the congregation has "peaked out," he says, at 7,000 attenders, "so we must build again."

The church resorted to two morning services only after they were absolutely forced into it. First they took out the children and put them in "children's church through high school." When they still ran out of space, they had no choice but to have an additional service.

Pastor Lindsay said, "We won't go to three services." They will begin building a third sanctuary in 1991. The new 9,200-seat auditorium will cost $15,400,000.

Lindsay was asked if the congregation had any difficulty accepting the idea of building a facility that would seat 9,200, when they had just completed a new auditorium 12 years earlier.

He answered, "We didn't begin soon enough." He explained that the people had to see that the auditorium was too small.

The church already had approximately $7 million when work began on the 9,200-seat auditorium. And because they pay cash and never borrow, it will take about three years to build; construction will go on as the money comes in. The church does not have special building fund campaigns, nor is a stewardship consultant hired to raise funds for new buildings.

Both Vines and Lindsay are optimists, so they support one another in future plans and future programs. "I am extremely high on the future of our church," Vines says. "I really do not believe there is any limitation on our ability to continue to grow and reach people. If we will keep our focus on Jesus and keep after the lost, we can continue to grow."

7

A NEW FACE FOR TRADITIONAL WORSHIP

Central Community Church
Wichita, Kansas

Rev. Ray Cotton, Pastor

THE CENTRAL COMMUNITY CHURCH OF WICHITA, KANSAS IS A FASCINAT-
ing and highly successful contradiction in terms; it is both
innovative and traditional. And embodying both these qualities in
his person is Central's pastor, Ray Cotton. His originality and creativity mark him as an innovative minister who provides his
church with the sort of up-to-date leadership strategy that typifies
Boomer-style churches today.

And though quite traditional in many respects, his church
offers worship with a flair and ministry with a functional twist. It
succeeds in combining these with an outstanding educational program and a small-group/cell ministry that is indeed unique.

Several phrases of the '90s describes changes at Central Community Church that make it a forward-looking congregation:

- First, the church uses a marketing strategy that focuses
  on people's needs.
- Second, its leadership is oriented toward research and
  innovation.
- Third, it targets "reachable" groups, based on a profile of
  the community and using direct mail, radio, television
  and other media on a regular basis to target those reachable segments of the community.
- Fourth, it has developed a strategy of evangelism based
  on relationships.
- Fifth, it is committed to helping members discover and
  use their spiritual gifts in ministry and in living the Christian life.

And underneath all this, the church is committed to excellence—the hallmark of Baby Boomers.

Two outward and controversial changes have occurred recently at Central Community Church: (1) dropping the name "Church of God, Anderson, Indiana," and (2) moving from the center of the city to a location four miles west of downtown in a primarily residential area. These external changes, however, reflect internal changes that are worth our noting in detail.

Change in Worship Style

Central Community Church is a "platform church." Yet it is not built on the charismatic personality of Senior Pastor Ray Cotton, but on the style of worship offered to its people. One member said, "We have changed from singing hymns to experiencing worship."

Music with Content

While the church uses praise choruses as an expression of worship, it has not departed from traditional classical music, nor from traditional hymns. George Skramstad, pastor of Worship and Arts, directs an orchestra—not a contemporary music band—of over 20 pieces that puts fire in the worship service. The people have the freedom to clap, and some lift their hands as they might do in a charismatic church.

The congregation sings from a nondenominational hymnbook. On Sunday evening they commit a large portion of the service to praise choruses and praise hymns. If praise choruses are used on Sunday morning, it may be in conjunction with traditional hymns, a solid anthem from the choir, a contemporary litany or a drama. It may even be followed by Bach or Handel as an offertory—and all this may have followed a prelude which incorporated a gospel song interpreted with a "big band" sound.

According to George Skramstad, the basis of worship is trust. He feels people must trust one another and the worship leadership to allow for any change in worship. Inasmuch as worship is subjective, he says, "We must be something for everyone." As a result they have contemporary music for the young, classical for the traditional and praise choruses for the charismatic; yet they are not married to any one type of worship.

Skramstad thinks charismatics are tired of the lack of "text and content" in worship, and desire to return to the traditional strength of liturgy. He finds charismatics want to sing the great hymns that express the church's theological heritage. "They want to sing something more than just simplistic testimony choruses."

Skramstad would like to see a complete range of art forms in worship, that is, the use of paintings, sculpture, dance, drama and quality multimedia. Although he says the church has been afraid of these forms, they "have brought me further into worship than incorporating faddish ideas."

Senior Pastor Ray Cotton testifies that in 1974 the church's worship was old-fashioned, which meant they sang hymns with feeling, but there was not always a coordinated worshiping theme. He also says that songs were often sung for their rhythm, not to develop a focused attention on God. "We never took time to ask why we were singing a song."

The Choir as Worship Leaders

Many charismatic churches have done away with the choir. Some charismatic leaders sarcastically describe the "choir box" as the place where people are put in a pen and not given the freedom to worship. However, at Central Community Church the choir is seen as worship leaders, with all music flowing from it.

As for solos, Skramstad says, "Unless soloists will plug into the entire team, I would rather they not sing solos." This means a person must be a member of the choir to sing a solo. When one does not willingly become a part of the entire music ministry team, but takes on the attitude of being a star performer, Skramstad says confusion is brought into the spirit of worship; the performer becomes the center of focus rather than Christ.

Although this does not exclude the use of guest artists, it is a general rule on which Skramstad is firm. He tells the story of a person, not in the choir, who walked into his office and said, "God put a solo on my heart to sing in church."

[Central Community] is need-centered, people-centered and worship-centered. The goal is to enable every person to experience the presence of God and stand in awe of His holiness.

"That's funny, God hasn't put it in my heart for you to sing," he responded.

The worshiper is the most important ingredient in the worship service at Central Community—not the soloist, choir, orchestra or even the pastor. The church is need-centered, people-centered and worship-centered. The goal is to enable every person to experience the presence of God and stand in awe of His holiness.

Worship Language, Liturgy and Excellence

The language of the worship folder reflects the change in the church's emphasis. They do not have a "platform" but a "chancel," and the choir is not just a "choir" but a "chancel choir." They do not have a "bulletin," but a "worship folder." Ray Cotton brings a "message," not a "sermon." And the "church building" is referred to as a "ministry center."

The church follows the liturgical calendar. While recognizing in a limited way special emphases such as Mother's Day, Father's

Day or the fourth of July, the focus of worship is always Christ. "We worship Christ," says Skramstad. Central Community Church wants to confirm the worship of God and His Son.

Excellence in every aspect of worship is a must at Central Community Church. "The world always has its best foot forward in the arts, in the concert halls and in technical areas. Now the church must also do its best. Special music and presentations must be memorized. The technical supports have to have the best quality and equipment. This is now a decade of expected excellence. That same quality must be present in worship if we are to survive," says Skramstad.

Change in Preaching Style

Pastor Ray Cotton testifies, "Over the years, I have changed my preaching style as a natural outcome of my growth in ministry." He tries to be relevant to the needs of the unchurched in his Sunday morning message. "I have developed a relational style to help people," he says. If the unchurched attend, he wants them to feel the presence of the Lord, yet at the same time he wants them to know that, as a pastor, he cares for them and their problems. He believes relevance, care and friendship will cause them to come back.

"I've stopped preaching and have begun speaking to people," Cotton says. To emphasize this goal, he comes out from behind the pulpit and stands in front of the people. Instead of telling them what to do, he shares with them in a conversational tone. "I'm not giving orders but talking with friends," he says.

When analyzing the change in his preaching, Cotton says, "Maybe I haven't changed that much. I've always seen myself as helpful. The seed was there. But as I saw the results of other communicators, it was natural for me to become more relational, positive and practical in my preaching." His people say that when Cotton preaches, his humble attitude comes through.

Change of Name

One of the most difficult things to change is the name of a church, especially when it is a traditional Church of God, Anderson, Indiana. One of the members testified, "Pastor Cotton didn't think it could happen." When he first talked about changing the name, a straw poll was taken and there was not enough support. One day a board member said to him, "Ray it is not that the people are against you, you are just so far ahead of them in their thinking."

Cotton waited two years. Meanwhile, he gave more of his energy to changing the church's ministry than changing the church's name. Many came to feel that the denominational name was a barrier to reaching the unchurched. When the church no longer saw itself as a traditional Church of God, but as a church that would minister to the whole community with innovative methods—yet not changing its message, then they were ready to change their name.

Now, although the legal name is still Central Community Church of God, the denominational tag "Church of God" is left off of advertisement and publicity. Yet the ties to the Church of God are as strong as ever. The new name is reflective of an open attitude to the community; it is truly a community church. When the vote finally came to change the name, only two families left the church over it.

Change of Location

It took over three years to bring the church to accept a change of location. This happened between 1979-1982. The church voted in 1983 to buy land, but it took four years before they were prepared to build on it. When the idea was first taken to the board, many did not want to talk about it.

A viability study was done, outlining the potential of ministry if the church was moved. The viability study directed the church toward the west side of Wichita. The leadership went on a retreat to discuss relocation, but many didn't show up.

It was difficult to get the people to talk about the move. Cotton finally came to the attitude, "I didn't care if we relocated or not as long as we were going to do something in ministry. I wasn't willing to retire at age 32 and do nothing."

At first the decision was made to buy property around the old location. A church building and old houses adjacent to the downtown location became available for $1.5 million. But they would have had to tear down some of the facilities for a parking lot.

Then Cotton advised the board that they could buy a large acreage on the west side of town near the freeway and across from a large regional shopping mall for the same price that they could buy the small acreage and buildings next to them downtown. The board approved buying the large acreage unanimously.

When the church voted on the move, an 85 percent majority approved. When they finally came to vote on building a new ministry center, a 95 percent majority favored it. When they finally moved into the new facilities, the church lost fewer than 25 families, most of whom lived on the city's east side and felt it was too far to come all the way across Wichita. The fact is, the church has become a regional church, with people driving from as far as two hours away, and its numbers are greatly increasing.

Attitude Toward Change

"Pastor Cotton doesn't push his ideas on us," a member at Central Community Church told me. "Not everything he does happens quickly. He introduces an idea and waits for people to think it through, then he gets it through."

His favorite phrase is "We will not make you do anything."

But the bottom line of why the church is characterized by innovation and change was reflected in a board member's observation: "This church will change more in the future because of Pastor Cotton's attitude than because of his methods."

One member said, "Change has come to Central Community Church because of freedom. The pastor has given me freedom to do it."

Another member said, "I don't think of change, I just do what is necessary. When we see what we must do, we naturally follow and I don't think of it as change."

As Pastor Ray Cotton was questioned for this book about change in the church, he replied, "I didn't realize how much had changed in the past 15 years since I became pastor."

But after giving it more thought he said, "I think things will change more in the future." However, change is never made for the sake of change. Cotton said, "If there is something not working, let's fix it."

Cotton knows that not all change is biblical or effective. He encourages his leadership to ask Why? and What happened?

Pastor Cotton has also encouraged his leadership to visit other churches on their vacations, to see how other churches operate, and whether different methods are effective. And, over the years, he himself has visited Robert Schuller at the Crystal Cathedral, Jack Hayford at the Church On The Way and many other churches to study their methods and approaches.

Organization and Structure

Whereas the church was committee-oriented when Ray Cotton came, a board member says, "Now we have a pastor-led church." This doesn't mean they have done away with committees or that the pastor works around committees to get his way. Rather, Cotton goes through committees. As a matter of fact, one of the strengths of the church is that Cotton knows how to work with committees.

At the same time, some of the committees that were not functioning properly were done away with. In their place managers or staff members were appointed to carry out their tasks. The committees on Christian education, youth, evangelism and missions were eliminated. They have restructured the work so that a pastor is accountable for each of those areas. That pastor sits with other pastors in the pastoral staff meeting. Although Ray Cotton attends, Mark Diffenbaugh is the moderator of that meeting.

All of the church's senior-level pastors sit on the church council. This council includes 12 lay council members and seven pastors, who set policies and approve the budget before it is submitted to the church. The people vote on their budget, and they vote on their senior pastor. After that the senior pastor carries out the program, and all staff members are responsible to him.

The question was asked, "How did this change happen?" As people resigned or left, new and more exciting options were created. As the staff grew they took over responsibility for the areas of ministry. New directions are outlined when the pastor gives a message on the state of the church at the end of each year. The people are excited, and they sit expectantly as he shares the goals for the coming year.

Change at Community Church therefore comes from a dream not a directive. When working toward changing the church's organization Cotton never said, "Let's change the structure of the church." Instead, he constantly referred to changing the vision by enlarging it. He spoke not of changing the basic nature of the church, but only of changing its vision and enlarging its ministry.

TLC Small Groups

One of Pastor Cotton's visions is of 10,000 people in worship, with 1,000 small Tender Loving Care (TLC) groups. So the church instituted a cell ministry called TLC groups, following the example of Dale Galloway at the New Hope Community Church, Portland, Oregon (see chapter 4). Ray Cotton realized that if he were going to revitalize his church, small groups were the way to build relationships, bond people to the church and involve them in ministry.

To begin the program, Cotton explained the need and the priorities of small groups and pushed to get them started. He hand-picked 50 people to come to his home once a week for three months as he trained them to lead small groups. He felt if the small groups were to succeed, his group leaders must do it out of conviction, and that this would only come about by experiencing a small group.

The success of Central Community is that they happen to organize [small groups] friends, give them a purpose and let them minister to one another.

The 50 leaders were organized into four groups, led by himself, his wife and two pastors on his staff. After three months, Ray asked, "Are you interested in being involved? Will you host a TLC small group, or will you lead one?" Those who agreed to do so were designated "lay pastors," and a commissioning service for them was held during a main service. They knelt at the altar, and hands were laid on them to commission them for this new ministry.

Presently, the TLC groups meet on different days and nights of the week, all studying the same curriculum to give the cell ministry structure and continuity. Support groups and specialty groups which are part of the program have their own specialized curriculum. There must be three persons to start a TLC group—usually a host, a leader and an assistant leader.

Members are free to leave the group when they wish and to

Central Community Church, Wichita, Kansas

fellowship with other groups. Groups usually have no more than 20 people in them, although one has over 30. They have a telephone network, follow up on prospects, give pastoral care and have an extensive prayer ministry for the needs of individuals.

The TLC groups begin with about 20 minutes of praise and worship, involving singing, testimony and sharing with one another. Next, they spend some 35 minutes studying the Word and making practical application. Finally, a 20-minute period is dedicated to prayer time, in which they again share, pray for one another and lay hands on those who need healing, restoration or other blessings.

A visitor is invited to a TLC group within a week after first walking into the church. If they get involved they immediately begin making friends. Some have observed that new people who go to TLC groups know more people in the church than some who have been in the church five years but are not in a group.

Senior lay pastors coordinate the small group districts and are accountable to the pastors. A person must be a lay pastor for at least two years before being promoted to coordinate several groups. At the beginning, the full-time pastors were district supervisors who gave oversight to the groups. At this writing, there are approximately 65-70 groups with around 800-900 people involved.

Cotton says that small groups are the glue that keep many people in Central Community Church. He said with an infectious grin, "All churches have small groups—they are called friends." The success of Central Community is that they happen to organize friends, give them a purpose and let them minister to one another.

Other Programs

Central Community Church has never had a busing program, although its Sunday School has grown with the church. In earlier years the Sunday School was larger than the church. A very dynamic and innovative Christian education program has served as one of the growing edges. Approximately 75 percent of those in worship attend Sunday School also. A large, attractive and well-equipped nursery serves the many young families.

Fifty Sunday School classes serve all ages from small children to older adults, with specialty classes for singles, remarried, young married, college, career and mentally handicapped adults. The educational program goes beyond the Sunday morning class to seminars, training and advocacy programs. The program has even been recognized by the state government as an outstanding model.

The Center for Christian Growth, which meets midweek, offers classes in theology, doctrine, church history, Bible overview and study and practical training for volunteers.

The Family Life Counseling Center provides counseling and helpful resources as well as sponsoring creative seminars and family life activities. "Seminar Evangelism" reaches the unchurched through a nonthreatening environment, offering practical, everyday help based on biblical principles. Parenting, stress management, divorce recovery and grief management are just a few that are offered at various times.

The Family Life Seminar is an innovative way of getting people into the church through the Sunday School. One seminar, "Your Family Can Be Fun," offered during Sunday School, has attracted many to the church. Over 800 people attended this seminar in the fall of 1989, with approximately half of the attendees being first-time guests.

Rather than having a group called the "Adult Sunday School Class," Central has seminars on family enrichment, lay evangelism and self-image. Someone said, "If we can get a new couple into a seminar for three or four weeks, we also get their kids in the Sunday School. Then the parents will return because their kids will like it, and it will make a difference in their home."

Children are very important to the church also, and as a result it has one of the largest and finest education facilities for children in the nation. Teaching, caring for and loving these children are of utmost importance in the church's program, which is designed to instill in them the Christian values so important in their lives now and later. Also, without a first-class children's department it is felt that parents would soon be out the backdoor.

Over the Horizon

Ray Cotton sees small groups as the wave of the future for the church, rather than mass media or any other method of outreach. He believes that the future foundation of Central Community Church will continue to be its TLC groups.

Cotton also sees that the future of the church is with the Baby Boomers. He hears John Maxwell, John Wimber and other Boomer pastors and feels their strategy is the path of the '90s, leading into the next century.

"I am very optimistic that things will improve for our church," he says, believing that Central Community's brightest times lie in the future. He expects to see more people reached for Christ in the future than in the past, with the church perhaps reaching as many as 50,000 in attendance. To reach this level, Cotton believes they will need 4,000 to 5,000 small groups.

8

A FELLOWSHIP OF EXCITEMENT

**Second Baptist Church
Houston, Texas**

Dr. H. Edwin Young, Pastor

SECOND BAPTIST CHURCH CALLS ITSELF "THE FELLOWSHIP OF EXCITE-ment," and those visiting the church truly are excited about what is going on there. Stan Dare, transferred from South St. Louis, Missouri to Houston and was captivated on his first visit to Second Baptist Church. He enrolled as an usher, got involved in counseling and joined a prayer group.

When he phoned long-distance to tell his wife about the excitement of the church, she asked him to wait until she could sell their home in St. Louis and move to Houston before he joined. Six weeks later she arrived in Houston, visited Second Baptist and shared her husband's enthusiasm. She later became a full-time secretary for Dr. Jim DeLoach, associate pastor.

Growth Through Vision: Expansion by Faith

Second Baptist Church was organized on March 6, 1927, by a group of dedicated people in a public school on Louisiana Street in downtown Houston. The following year they purchased a former Methodist church and constructed some Christian education facilities.

Approximately 30 years later, the church acquired 25 acres at its present location on Woodway Drive in the Memorial area, a rapidly-growing part of southwest Houston. Four years later, two education facilities and a gymnasium were built, and the church's 1,300 members worshiped there until they could construct a sanctuary. A beautiful new sanctuary seating 1,450 was built in 1968.

In 1978, Dr. H. Edwin Young was called as pastor. He brought most of his staff with him from the First Baptist Church of Columbia, South Carolina, and the church began its upward, exponential rate of growth. Under Young's leadership, the church began multiple worship services, and worshipers spilled over the adjacent areas equipped with closed-circuit television. Over 9,000 people have joined Second Baptist Church in the past nine years, and its Sunday School attendance has grown more than 4,000 during the same period.

In 1983, with great vision, the church made a decision to build a new worship center, educational facilities and a family life center—a monumental $34 million undertaking. The worship center seats 6,200 but has the potential of accommodating 8,000. The choir loft alone seats 450.

The facility also houses conference rooms, choir rehearsal rooms equipped with recording sets, orchestra and rehearsal areas, a music library, 11 classrooms, a church parlor that will accommodate 300, a large multi-purpose room with a service kitchen, theater facilities for projection, a media room for audiovisual operations, a snack bar, a large fellowship garden, plus all of the recreational facilities of the Family Life Center.

When the church moved into its new facilities, it was one of the most expensive new church buildings constructed recently. Then immediately, still another piece of property became available. The church realized that if they didn't purchase the land, it might not be available again for many years, if at all.

The new piece of land had a $17 million price tag. That figure, plus the $34 million for the new facilities, made a total of $51 million—and this at a time when Houston's oil-based economy was struggling to survive. Oil prices were sliding, and oil millionaires were going into bankruptcy.

Yet the church made a decision to go forward and spend the extra funds. Young said, "All we bought was dirt, but it was necessary to secure any potential for expansion for the future."

As a result of their expansion program, the church owed $27 million in 1989—a staggering debt for any local church. They paid off $7 million, reducing the debt to approximately $20 million. While this still seems a massive debt, the church pledged a $12 million annual budget, plus an extra $7 million to reduce its indebtedness, making its total giving in one year $19 million! This budget is perhaps the largest of any local church in the country, excluding auxiliary ministries such as television, colleges and/or other ministries.

The facilities of the new worship center, dedicated in June 1986, include one of the most beautiful sanctuaries in the world. The six-story, massive stained glass windows to the right and left of the pulpit are the largest in the world. The Rodgers organ, with 10,473 pipes, is one of the largest in the world, with state-of-the-art components, including a laser disc computer which allows for totally accurate and instant replay.

But the traditional beauty of the new sanctuary does not mean that Second Baptist is a formal, liturgical church. It is a gospel-preaching church where people walk the aisle and are saved Sunday after Sunday.

Having built a sanctuary that seated 6,200, the church did not anticipate the need to go to two worship services so soon. But in a single year average worship attendance jumped by another 2,842 people a week, and they were putting chairs in the aisle to accommodate the overflow. With a $34 million building that was completely filled, double services were the most likely solution; so after only 14 months the church began two Sunday morning worship services, at 9:40 and 11 A.M.

An Innovative Sunday School

When the church built its new facilities and began to see exponential attendance growth, three Sunday School hours were scheduled—8:30, 9:40 and 11 A.M. The 8:30 hour is the largest. But there is more to Second Baptist's Sunday School than multiple meeting times and numbers in attendance. Innovation is also a hallmark of this Sunday School.

But innovation often means change and, as Young explains, "Some people get in a rut and hate to change, even when their ministry is not working." Consequently, to keep the Sunday School program invigorated and on the cutting edge, Young suggests that change for change's sake is sometimes necessary.

At the same time, to ensure that change is not without purpose and direction, Young emphasizes that "nothing happens at our church that is not programmed through the Sunday School." For example, an extensive prayer ministry is facilitated through the Sunday School. Evangelism programs, fellowships and even more than 50 softball teams are also organized and implemented through the Sunday School.

Larger Class Size

The program of Second Baptist's Sunday School has many characteristics of the balanced Sunday School program which was developed and introduced by Arthur Flake in his classic *Building a Standard Sunday School* (first published in 1922) and which is built on the laws of Sunday School growth. Yet the Sunday School is not typical Southern Baptist. Southern Baptists tend to keep their classes small, with approximately 10 in each class while Second Baptist may have between 20 and 200 in attendance.

Novel Adult Program

And most Southern Baptist churches divide even the adult classes by age and gender, but a unique approach to the division of classes, as well as careful assignment of teachers, are key factors in Second Baptist's success. Instead of assigning one teacher to a class, Second Baptist assigns two—usually a man and a woman— who teach on alternate Sundays.

Also, each class has a full slate of officers, including a director, outreach leader, social director, special projects coordinator, ministry network leader, discipleship coordinator, shepherd coordinator, shepherd leaders and prayer coordinators. The phenomenal growth at Second Baptist Church is built on equipping leadership such as this and involving lay people at every level of church ministry.

The Married Young Adult Division, ages 18 to 26, has six classes; Married Adult I, ages 27 to 31, has eight classes; Married Adult II, ages 32 to 36, six classes; Married Adult III, ages 37 to 48, nine classes; and Married Adult IV, age 49 and over, nine classes.

Pastor Young sees clearly the pressures secular society and the business community place on the family. So "we pitched our tent toward the family."

In addition to these age-graded adult classes, the Sunday School has special classes for new members, single parents, Spanish-speaking members, as well as classes on marriage enrichment, Bible characters, Bible doctrine and others.

Over 4,300 married adults are on the roll, with an average adult attendance of 3,350 each Sunday. The special classes have 963 members on their rolls, with approximately 700 in attendance weekly.

Extensive Singles Ministry

The singles ministry of Second Baptist Church is the largest in the nation, with an enrollment of over 3,600 and an average weekly attendance of 1,436—not surprising, perhaps, in a city in which 53 percent of the population are singles. Ten classes minister to singles from college age to age 26. Six classes exist for singles age 27 to 31, and six from ages 32 to 36. Another six classes are offered for the 36-and-over age group. Second Baptist is one of several other large Southern Baptist Churches—First Baptist, Tallowood

Baptist and Forest Baptist, all of Houston; and First Baptist, Jacksonville—with extensive singles ministry.

Strong Family Emphasis

Even with an extensive and well-known singles ministry, Pastor Ed Young set a family emphasis when he first came to the church. He sees clearly the pressures secular society and the business community place on the family. So after observing the other local churches and the needs of Second Baptist, Young says "we pitched our tent toward the family."

Young views the church as an "island" that families can retreat to often for fellowship, learning enrichment, service and play. The new $34 million addition to the campus includes a family life center with three gymnasiums, an eight-lane bowling alley, racquetball courts, billiards, game room, weight room, aerobics room, theater and crafts room. A snack bar/grill offers fellowship and physical replenishment.

Not surprisingly, Second Baptist Church is an exciting family church that seeks to minister to every area of its members' lives.

"Drafting" Lay Leaders

A few years ago on a staff retreat, Young asked, "What is the weakest area of our church?"

Nearly every staff member wrote down "lay involvement" as the weakest link in ministry.

Indeed, since the church had occupied its new facilities with little or no expansion of paid staff, the need for more lay involvement was crucial. The problem forced the leadership to become increasingly innovative in their recruiting efforts. Getting more lay people active in positions of leadership and, thereby, facilitating maximum use of the facilities were critical challenges.

So, in the fall of 1989, a "draft" was instituted to establish current and new Sunday School leadership. Just as sports teams draft players to meet their specific needs, members were drafted by directors to fill key spots in Sunday School classes. A large board with names of available workers gave each director an opportunity to draft those needed for his class. Draftees were chosen and then recruited by directors.

According to Young, the draft was a fantastic success. The enthusiasm generated by this approach epitomized the old Sunday School "rally" of years past. And one unexpected benefit of this creative project was the excitement it generated among laity for Sunday School.

Today laymen lead large committees involving hundreds of people in projects and special events each year. Many would suggest now that lay leadership is the strongest asset of Second Baptist Church.

Young agrees, saying, "We have turned it around."

A Year for the Unchurched

Each year the church adopts a certain theme, such as the "Year of Faithfulness," the "Year of Stewardship" or the "Year of Prayer." This year, 1990, is the "Year of Evangelism." The church's goal is to baptize 1,000 people in 1990. While it has taken in over 2,000 new members in a single year, baptizing as many as 767 in that time period, the church has never baptized 1,000.

"Think unchurched people," Young challenged his congregation. The moment visitors arrive on this campus, they find a system that is geared to the unchurched. There is music in the parking lot, names to identify parking areas, curbside greeters to open the car door, and valet parking for senior adults.

Church workers, including the pastoral staff, teachers and regular members, do not park on the church campus—there is no place for them. Those arriving at the 8:30 A.M. Sunday School are not allowed to park on campus at all, unless they are visitors.

Second Baptist Church, Houston, Texas

They drive to one of three remote parking areas where they board one of 22 shuttle buses to the church.

With 2,387 parking spaces on campus, and a little over that number just off campus, the church has parking for over 5,000 cars within a two-mile radius. Even the stoplights are coordinated to help get traffic to the church on Sunday mornings.

"Parking is our ongoing battle," says Young. It is a challenge this church is responding to with a spirit of cooperation.

To reach the unchurched, the church sponsors evangelistic outreach parties, some held in members' neighborhoods and some in particular zip code areas. These are held all over the city of Houston—with some as far as 30 miles away. Many hesitate to visit the church because of the traffic situation on Sunday, but they may be "networked" into the church through these neighborhood parties. These gatherings center on fellowship, but someone will share what the Lord has done in his or her life.

As a result, these people will come with friends to the church. Neighborhood evangelistic parties help remove the mental barrier from attending an unfamiliar church. They create a desire to experience the excitement of Second Baptist Church.

Consequently, the church reaches more than just Southern Baptists moving into Houston. As a matter of fact, they are primarily geared to reach those who are not Southern Baptists. One of the largest groups coming into the church consists of Roman Catholics. Also coming are Methodists, Presbyterians and other groups of Protestants.

A number of Jewish believers or "completed Jews" have also come into the church. This fellowship uses the nearest Hebrew word for excitement, which is *l'chaim*—a word that communicates excitement and expectancy. Even though the Hebrew word is traditionally used for a toast, Jews understand it and respond to it.

New members are assimilated by every possible means. If a person joins the church, they may receive as many as 13 phone calls within three weeks, along with five letters and perhaps two to three visits. The church does everything it can to get these new members into one of the Sunday School classes that are available to them. Young says, "We go after them because we believe they must be involved in every part of the body."

Thinking Ahead

The church goes forward on what has been called "ad hocology"—putting together lay committees outside the line and staff responsibilities. Young calls these bodies "think tanks." The church has formed approximately eight such think tanks to address its challenges and come up with suggestions and/or solutions.

Each think tank has up to 12-15 people who are given an assignment with definitive questions to answer. Such questions might be: How can we solve our parking problem? or How long do we use parking garages off campus? or How can we involve people who have recently come into our church?

Other Ministries

The Christian School
Second Baptist Church has a Christian school—kindergarten through grade 12—with 965 students enrolled. It has competitive football, basketball, soccer, baseball and track teams, and provides superior academic education.

Just as Charles Spurgeon had the "watches" that provided a prayer foundation for the great outreach of Metropolitan Baptist Tabernacle 100 years ago in London, Second Baptist Church is growing because of prayer.

An International Emphasis
The church also finds some of its flock gravitating toward its various international classes. Each Sunday morning the service is simultaneously translated into Spanish.

The MasterLife Program
The church is involved in the Southern Baptist MasterLife program, which is 26 weeks of basic discipleship designed to ground people in the Word of God. Young asked, "If you had 10,000 new babies and only 4,000 people to look after them, how would you do it?" He emphasizes the necessity of MasterLife in teaching discipleship to the new people who have come into the church.

Follow-up and Visitation
The church does not utilize traditional spring and fall revival meet-

ings, because they already have so many unchurched people coming through different "windows." Outreach leaders are assigned the task of following up on these people through the Sunday School. The pastoral staff is also involved in visitation. The 34 administrative staff members turn in a visitation report each week to Young, who provides them with feedback on their efforts.

Emphasis on Prayer

Young believes one reason for the explosive growth of this church is prayer. Just as Charles Spurgeon had the "watches" that provided a prayer foundation for the great outreach of Metropolitan Baptist Tabernacle 100 years ago in London, Second Baptist Church today is growing because of prayer. Two full-time staff members supervise the Prayer Ministry.

But Second Baptist does more than say prayer is important: *they pray.* More than praying at home, they come to the church to pray. To demonstrate the extent of their commitment, someone is praying at the church 24 hours a day, seven days a week, 365 days a year. Security guards watch the facilities all night.

Each year Second Baptist sponsors two churchwide Schools of Prayer. These schools help to develop the personal and corporate prayer life of the church by encouraging and motivating people to pray. The first School of Prayer is held in the spring, and is led by Dr. James R. DeLoach, associate pastor. There are sessions for personal Bible study, challenges and specified times for prayer.

The fall School of Prayer is led by a guest teacher who covers such topics as "God's Plan for Prayer Mobilization," "Prayer for Healing," "The Role of Prayer in Spiritual Awakening," "Prayer in Fasting" and "Equipping the Body of Christ to Pray." During a month of prayer emphasis, the church family is given an opportunity to sign up for an hour in the Prayer Room, where prayer is made 24 hours a day. There are testimonies, Bible Study classes and articles in the church newsletter to focus attention on prayer.

Once a year an annual prayer banquet is held to honor the faithfulness of the regular Prayer Room intercessors and volunteer workers in the Prayer Ministry. Those who have worked for five years in the Prayer Ministry receive special recognition at this banquet. It is a great time of sharing answers to prayer and giving thanks to God for His goodness to the church.

Twice each month a one-hour prayer orientation is held, teaching new members how to work and pray in the Prayer Room. Many phone calls coming to the church are funneled to the Prayer Room, where much of the church's pastoral care goes on. People may—and do—call at all times of the day and night. Someone is there to talk with them and, at the end of the call, to pray for them.

Many who are sick come to periodic chapel services where they are anointed (see James 5:14), hands are laid on them and people pray for their specific physical needs.

9

A NEW FACE FOR MINISTRY

Horizon Christian Fellowship
San Diego, California

Rev. Michael Kirk MacIntosh, Pastor

O N THE NEAR-NORTH SIDE OF SUBURBAN SAN DIEGO IS A UNIQUE AND innovative church spread over a 20-acre facility that was once a junior high school campus. It is Horizon Christian Fellowship, a church with a distinct ministry to young people—the average age is 28—that also includes all ages among the 4,000 to 5,000 people in average Sunday attendance. Its founder and present leader is Michael Kirk MacIntosh, 46, a native of Oregon who understands the life-style of rebellious young people because he experienced that rebellion in his 20s on the beaches of southern California.

Taking on the Devil for the Kids

Mike MacIntosh asks, "Who is going to lead the Church into the twenty-first century?" He is deeply concerned about the explosion of the drug culture in American society and claims that very few people in our day are seriously interested in relating to urban youth. He points out that on the streets of our cities are 3.1 million teens who have either run away from home or have been disenfranchised by their families. "There must be a fresh, new ministry to reach them" he says.

"When I survey the territory today I see the devil leading our nation's young people to hell in huge numbers," MacIntosh says. "Someone has got to come up with new ideas, new programs and a new vision to reach them with the transforming message of Jesus Christ." He cites the drug culture as one of the major problems, if not *the* major problem, facing youth in America. He notes that a large segment of the younger generation listens to drug-inspired music, watches drug-affirming movies and cruises around in cars with friends who require a "high" just to be able to talk to one another.

"No one is taking on the devil for the kids, but I'd like to pick up the challenge," says Mike MacIntosh. His Youth Development International (YDI) program, a national hotline for teens to phone in and talk to other teens, has experienced a rapid growth in telephone responses over the past two years. With the advertising of the 800 phone number in commercial movies, on television and in other media exposures, including the Goodyear blimp, the ministry has virtually exploded. In 1986 YDI took 30,000 phone calls from youths. That figure jumped to 139,000 in 1987 to 180,000 in 1988 and to 250,000 in 1989.

MacIntosh claims to have the "only Christian national hotline with born-again kids answering the phones." Thus, when a teen phones in, most of the time the one answering prays with him or her, asking the caller to receive Jesus into his or her heart. Often the caller is referred to churches or shelters for troubled youth in his or her area.

MacIntosh is a chaplain to the San Diego Police Department and a member of the San Diego Crime Commission. Because he has come out of the drug world himself, he has a deep compassion for hurting kids. He knows that many of the nation's problems show up in the phone calls: "My dad raped me....I have just shot drugs....My pimp has locked me up...." One teenage male prostitute called to say that he was in trouble with his pimp and feared that the pimp had killed his brother. He was told, "Get out of there immediately."

From Beach Bum to Born-Again Christian

Mike MacIntosh himself could have died in the drug culture during the late 1960s. He lived as a beach bum, charming the society girls vacationing in southern California, but dating them only if they paid for the dinner. He experimented with every drug known to the rock musicians in those days. If he overdosed, he found that his friends fell by the wayside.

On one occasion he suffered an LSD-induced hallucination and thought that someone had blown away half his head with a gun. He went through the terrifying conviction that he was dead. His drug-inflamed imagination drove him into the high California desert, where he scanned the skies looking for UFOs.

He bummed around with friends who practiced Yoga, Zen and Satan-worship. On one occasion he was chanting in the predawn when he heard a sharp crack like a bullwhip. He later decided it was a drug reaction, but it became for him "the crack of dawn" on a new life.

After one drug-filled weekend bumming around with friends, Mike went to the Laguna Beach police to relate a wild story about how the Beatles were in town and he had joined their group. After listening to him, the police escorted him to the Orange County Medical Center, where he was placed in a holding tank with several other patients. His case was evaluated by a psychiatrist, then by a full psychiatric board. He was diagnosed as a paranoid schizophrenic.

After four years as a "free spirit," living on the beaches of southern California, Mike MacIntosh, a good-looking young man who appeared to have everything, had reached the end of the line. He said later of those days, "I couldn't have been more miserable." His marriage had ended in divorce, he was in difficulties with the law, in debt and under psychiatric treatment.

On his twenty-sixth birthday, MacIntosh was invited by friends to attend a musical service at Calvary Chapel in Costa Mesa. That night the gospel was preached, and Mike took Jesus Christ as his Savior. The nightmare was over; he had found Someone to follow.

In his book, *For the Love of Mike*, Sherwood Eliot Wirt, founder of the San Diego County Christian Writers' Guild and former editor of Billy Graham's magazine, *Decision*, told the gripping story of

Horizon Christian Fellowship, San Diego, California

MacIntosh's conversion from a life of frustration and defeat. He quotes Mike: "If I could come back after being so far down, then Jesus Christ can do the same for any other person." Out of the pit came the foundation of a new life, a new church and a worldwide ministry.

For five years after his salvation, Mike worked under Pastor Chuck Smith at Calvary Chapel, whose church had drawn thousands of similar young men and women to Jesus Christ. The Chapel became a mecca for the "Jesus Generation," and the near-by Pacific Ocean became the site of mass baptisms. Today hundreds of similar Calvary Chapels have been established all over North America by young men who found their Lord in Costa Mesa.

Under Pastor Smith's guidance, MacIntosh moved into a "commune" for training in the Christian life. It was a boarding house with Christian standards and fellowship that included Bible study, discipline and hard work. In this spiritual boot camp, MacIntosh and his colleagues spent time in the Bible morning, noon and night. They learned how to take up the cross, how to get along with others, how to witness and how to earn a living. This commune, which they dubbed "Mansion Messiah," proved more effective than many Bible schools. Later Mike joined the staff at Calvary Chapel and was ordained.

MacIntosh developed rapidly in his ministerial training, and had the joy of seeing his divorced wife, Sandra, brought to Christ. She had been impressed by the change in Mike's life-style. After living apart for three years, they sensed the Lord calling them to put their marriage back together. Pastor Smith performed the ceremony. Today instead of the two children they had when their lives drifted apart, they have five beautiful children, some of them now grown.

From Music to Ministry

After being a high school dropout, MacIntosh resumed his education and received Master of Ministry and Master of Divinity degrees from the Graduate School of Theology at Azusa Pacific University.

Before he established his present ministry in San Diego, MacIntosh spent several years as director of Maranatha Music. Under his leadership this organization pioneered in the contemporary Christian praise music which has won popularity around the world.

In 1974 Mike was invited by friends to teach a weekly Bible class. It began with 12 people in a private home on Point Loma, and soon expanded to 45 enthusiastic young converts. In August of that year, the group moved to the Ocean Beach Women's Club, where 60 people gathered. Soon over 100 were studying the Bible, and they moved to Balboa Park, where they began holding Sunday services in the House of Hospitality.

By this time MacIntosh was adding communication and

preaching skills to the management abilities he had acquired at Maranatha. In 1975 the young congregation moved to an unused church facility in the Linda Vista area of San Diego. In addition to young people, families began attending. When the old North Park theater, with a seating capacity of 1,200, became available the following year, the group purchased and renovated it. The ever-growing crowd now required three Sunday services, two in the morning and one in the evening.

The secret of church growth, MacIntosh believes, is "the right means, in the right culture, in the right place, at the right time, with the right people receptive."

Horizon Christian Fellowship Is Born

MacIntosh's vision continued to expand. During the fall of 1976 the fellowship planted its first mission church in San Diego's North County. By 1980, nine churches had grown out of the original fellowship, in the communities of Encinitas, El Cajon, Escondido, Chula Vista, Poway, Pacific Beach, Point Loma and Alpine. MacIntosh changed the name "Calvary Chapel" to "Horizon Christian Fellowship."

The new ministry of Horizon was committed to winning people to Christ, discipling them, then sending them out to reach others for Christ. The church built a family center across the street from the North Park Theater. The staff grew. And a ministry to the deprived and homeless was added.

Horizon International Ministries

Horizon International Ministries was launched to carry out the church's worldwide mission. Mike and Sandy traveled abroad, and saw fresh opportunities to serve the Lord in the countries of Europe and Asia.

MacIntosh has traveled the world, conducting evangelistic crusades in Scotland, Mexico, the Philippines, Grenada and many American cities. His church has spearheaded major relief efforts with food, medicine, clothing and emergency assistance in such places as Uganda, Poland, the Philippines and Mexico. In the Soviet Union, MacIntosh helped in the release of Siberian evangelicals who had spent seven years as refugees in the basement of the American embassy in Moscow.

Horizon School of Evangelism

In a day when many large churches are establishing their own Bible schools and colleges to train leaders, MacIntosh has taken a different route. "I don't see much effective leadership coming out of the seminaries," he said. He prefers the path he took into his own ministry.

His aim is to get a young convert away from the city drug life. He finds the biggest obstacles facing the convert are fornication, lack of discipline and getting along with others. Young people who grow up in a drug-oriented society, he says, have no purpose, no motivation and no ability to give themselves to other people.

For that reason the Horizon School of Evangelism has established three wilderness experience trips during the year, so young people can learn how to fend for themselves and how to live with one another. Such trips are usually to Death Valley, the High Sierras or Catalina Island. They are given a chance to exist by themselves for 48 hours, taking care of necessities with bare essentials. They have their own sleeping bags and cooking utensils.

For many, the experience will be useful when they go out on an evangelistic mission in a foreign country, since they will not book into posh hotels but unroll their sleeping bags on church pews. In this unique way, the founding of the Horizon School of Evangelism has given the church an international outreach focus, as hundreds of young people have been trained for ministry and mobilized to travel with MacIntosh on his evangelistic and mercy missions. So though the Horizon School of Evangelism was launched to help city young people mature socially and spiritually, it also helps train these same young people in missionary outreach.

Style Changes and Continuing Growth

In 1985 Horizon was able to lease its present site, the 20-acre former junior high school campus, from the city of San Diego. By this time, weekly attendance was averaging 2,500, and the church had planted 14 other churches and ordained 33 pastors. With city permission, Horizon built a $1.5 million gymnasium, in which it now worships.

The secret of church growth, MacIntosh believes, is "the right means, in the right culture, in the right place, at the right time, with the right people receptive." He had watched the growth of Calvary Chapel, Costa Mesa, under the ministry of Chuck Smith during the Vietnam War years. That was when hallucinogenic drugs were first coming into wide popularity, when flags were being burned, governments were distrusted and free love and free speech had become the life-style of millions of young people.

Innovative techniques, ways of meeting kids on the beach, winning them to Christ and baptizing them in the ocean, were popular. Thousands of young people were reached. However, as Horizon Christian Fellowship grew, it changed its original orientation, which was heavily based on music and had its strong roots in the beach culture.

So the church no longer caters primarily to beach kids. Business people, servicemen, college students and blue-collar laborers make up much of the membership. Many were formerly drug people. All races are liberally represented among both the staff and membership.

The mainstream of San Diego residents seem to feel at home with the style of worship offered at Horizon. As noted, the congregation's average age is 28. Forty-nine percent of those attending are single, and one-half are men

Conversions are still an important base of the church's growth, but it is now drawing on its own Sunday School as well. The young "hippies" have married, and biological church growth is taking place.

Also, many people are coming to Horizon because they are dissatisfied with the "business as usual" attitude in their own churches. Dissatisfied liberals are finding a clear gospel ministry at Horizon. Fundamentalists are finding release from legalistic attitudes in which they grew up. Pentecostals are finding solid Bible teaching instead of emotionalism.

Horizon has found a niche in the Christian community where other churches are not ministering, and the result is continuous, steady growth. Prior to moving into its present facility, Horizon had not been perceived by many Christians as a genuine church body, but rather as a youth evangelistic ministry. Today that is no longer true. The Sunday School and the Christian day school have brought institutional stability, as more mature Christians continue to bring their families from other churches.

Casual dress has always been a characteristic of worship at Horizon, as people enjoy being comfortable while they worship and study the Bible. When the author attended a prayer meeting, he was the one out of 700 worshipers with a white shirt and tie. But this church is located in southern California, and it maintains a delicate balance between dignity and comfort, between form and function.

No Televangelism or Supersanctuary

Television, MacIntosh feels, is not necessarily the best medium for evangelism or worship, because the Church is alien to the world and speaks a language unfamiliar to a secular audience. He himself used television nationwide for three years, but went off the air rather than beg for money. He feels that by using so much airtime for fund-raising, religion wears out its welcome. The typical televangelist turns people off, Mike believes.

"For evangelism to be effective, people must gather where the dynamic of the Spirit of God is present, and the people by and large do not feel that dynamic when they watch television."

Neither does MacIntosh have any intention of building a massive sanctuary. He has spoken to vast stadium crowds, once giving his testimony at a Billy Graham outdoor crusade meeting in Anaheim. He knows how difficult it is to maintain personal eye contact with people when preaching to more than 5,000.

"I'd rather have three services at 5,000 each than to have 10,000 or 15,000 at one time," he says.

Home Fellowship Groups

Horizon Church does not have an official membership and, therefore, people never join. However, when people start attending regularly, they are invited to become accountable to a home fellowship group, to tithe regularly and to become actively involved in ministry.

The Key to Horizon's Ministry

The home fellowship group, which in many ways is the key to the church's ministry, has four levels of structure. A home fellowship director oversees the entire group structure. Assisting the director are 16 area leaders, and assisting them are sectional leaders who minister to the groups in their section. Finally, home fellowship leaders are responsible for the individual groups. Nearly half of the Sunday worshipers are active in home fellowships. The goal is 100 percent.

The Means of Horizon's Growth

The growth of Horizon church from 3,000 to 5,000 attendees in 1989 was brought about by the expansion of the home fellowship groups. When the 62 groups were increased to 90, the new groups

---

Mike MacIntosh says, "By nature I like change." His church was not a typical church when it was first planted; radical changes have taken place over the years...and have come out of vision.

---

impacted the church by nearly a thousand new adults and a thousand new children. Today the church averages over 5,500 in attendance each weekend, with a Saturday evening service recently added to the two Sunday morning services.

The Format of the Groups

What happens in a home fellowship group? Each begins with singing and worship, followed by a Bible study following an assigned text. During 1990 the groups will be studying the book of Acts and Paul's letters to the Philippians, Romans and Ephesians. After the Bible study there are times of prayer and testimony, as well as times when pastoral care is administered by the leader and by individuals to each other.

The Way to Reach Others

MacIntosh believes there are probably more witches than clergymen in his city. The number of cult-related crimes in San Diego is rising at an alarming rate. But he finds many clergymen are totally ignorant as to what is happening among the cults today.

He is concerned about cultic influence because he once lived in that world. He believes that small groups gathering for Bible study are the best way to reach not only those who are caught up in the occult, but other people as well; and that the churches that use such groups are the effective churches.

Attitude Toward Change

Mike MacIntosh says, "Change is my middle name. By nature I like change." His church was not a typical church when it was first planted, and radical changes have taken place over the years. He says the changes have come out of vision.

He believes the pastor must lead the church with prophetic vision. "I love to read the prophets," he explained, "and learn how they spoke to their generation. They understood the pitfalls the people faced, and tried to correct their faults."

MacIntosh makes no apologies for focusing on reaching youth at the beaches when he was younger, nor does he apologize now for seeking to reach the suburban, married Boomers. "I don't speak primarily to my mother's generation. At first I became impatient with people who couldn't see what I saw. I doubted if they really wanted to change."

Just as some traditional churches must change to meet the needs of people as they grow and mature, so MacIntosh, who began with a dozen long-haired young people in a Bible study, had to shift emphasis toward a more traditional approach. "I had to slow down," he says, "so the people could catch the vision."

When he first began to pastor, MacIntosh says, he gave orders. Now he sees the necessity for being a leader rather than simply the boss of the church. "I must first communicate my vision to the people, and give them a dream of what they can do. Then I work with them as they work out the vision. My management of the vision must become their management. Then I must go on to the next project."

Where new followers of Christ begin with physical changes and move to spiritual change, Mike feels the leader must take the opposite tack. He must start with a vision of spiritual change and then move to physical change. "The street kids must be established as parents of their kids." He believes that the typical church today is not relating to the radical young or the institutional young, and it must change if it is to stay in existence.

Over the Horizon

What of the future? In an interview, MacIntosh said, "I see the first American atheistic generation just over the horizon." That was by way of explaining why he named his new church "Horizon."

He added, "We are creating a society that has never been told that God made the universe. Children reared in humanism grow up with a strong defense mechanism toward the church. A people without God are doomed to fight World War III. That is what I see over the horizon."

MacIntosh also says, "I have discovered in recent years a growing disillusionment with the evangelistic church as a result of the PTL and Jimmy Swaggart scandals." He has made his church a tight ship, committed to godliness, discipline and "servant leadership." And he plans to keep it that way.

Horizon also plans to outgrow its present quarters soon. Pastor MacIntosh's next goal is 240 home fellowship cells, which would produce 3,000 people. Such small cells originally grew out of the Sunday services, but now it appears that the reverse is happening: the cell groups produce larger Sunday services. Because of the potential infrastructure of the cells, MacIntosh envisions a weekend attendance of 12,000 at the worship services.

He adds drily, "If Horizon hadn't started 14 other congregations, we could have 15,000 to 20,000 people in our services now!"

10
ONE CHURCH IN TWO LOCATIONS

Mount Paran Church of God
Atlanta, Georgia

Dr. Paul Walker, Pastor

MOUNT PARAN CHURCH OF GOD WAS NOT THE FIRST CONGREGATION to minister from two locations, but perhaps no other church has done it so effectively. Technically called a "Geographically Extended Parish Church" (see chapter 16), the 10,000-member church gives innovative meaning to the phrase, "Multiple pastors, multiple ministries and multiple places of ministry." While Dr. Paul L. Walker is the senior pastor and driving force behind this extended outreach, he has over 200 people who minister with him as staff and pastors.

In 1989 contributions at Mount Paran totalled $10,885,679, giving it one of the largest budgets among American churches. But its numerical growth in the past few years is what has given it national significance. The church has grown by about 4,000 weekly attenders since extra worship services were added at an additional location called Mount Paran North.

A History of Growth

The church was originally organized in the summer of 1918 as the first congregation representing the Church of God, Cleveland, Tennessee, in the Atlanta area. In the early days several churches merged to form the Hemphill Church of God near the University of Georgia Tech campus in the near northside of downtown Atlanta. In 1960, Dr. Paul L. Walker was serving as a state Christian education and youth director for the Church of God. A pastoral search committee for the Hemphill Church of God interviewed him at their national assembly, and after earnest prayer Dr. Walker accepted the call and leadership of the church.

When the Hemphill church property was acquired by Georgia Tech, the church purchased six acres on Mount Paran Road in the far northside of Atlanta, approximately six miles away. The name

Mount Paran North

Mount Paran Central

of the church was changed to Mount Paran Church of God, and the first service was held in the $850,000 complex on July 9, 1967. Within two years, the church was making plans for an expansion of facilities and, more importantly, an expansion of ministries. In the next 10 years, several new ministries were added, such as

---

Paul Walker defines worship as the total expression of the heart to God in adoration and praise. Worship is the "high water mark" of the believer's experience.

Mount Paran Christian School (K-12), and the Psychological Studies Institute, an adjunct program in Christian Counseling at Georgia State University, offering a Master's degree in counseling.

In 1987 the church reached what Dr. Walker calls a breakthrough in its expansion and outreach. The church had grown so large on Mount Paran Road that there was absolutely no more room to build. Parking was saturated, they were busing people by shuttle from other parking lots and they had as many Sunday worship services (three) as humanly possible. It was not feasible to build a parking deck to use one day a week, so Dr. Walker began praying about other ministries and other forms of outreach.

The answer came in August 1987, when the property and facilities of Marietta Baptist Tabernacle became available. For $3.5 million, Mount Paran Church of God acquired 65 acres of property and 120,000 square feet of buildings, including an auditorium that seated 3,500. It then had to secure an additional $9 million for 10 more acres, 30,000 square feet of additional educational space, landscaping, parking and renovation. (Even though they acquired a church building, they had to meet all of the new existing building codes.) The church raised $5 million in cash and borrowed $7 million dollars for the new facility, called Mount Paran North Church. It now meets in two locations, separated by 14.5 miles, mostly expressway driving.

Now the church has a 9 A.M. service at Mount Paran North with approximately 3,000 in attendance, and an evening service at 6 P.M. with approximately 500 in attendance. The congregation also has an early morning service at Mount Paran Road at 7:45 A.M., when communion is served to approximately 200 people. Sunday services at Mount Paran Road (called Mount Paran Central) are at 9 and 11 A.M., and 7:00 P.M., making six services each Sunday in two locations.

Profile of the Pastor

Paul Walker is a native son of the Church of God, Cleveland, Tennessee. He hopes to form a model church that is committed to his denomination, yet one that does not become just like them in philosophy of ministry. At one time the church felt ostracized by its denomination for its innovative methods. Yet no one could deny the church's growth (10 percent a year for 10 years.) Now Dr. Walker and the church are used by the denomination in various avenues of training so that it is more than an "example"; it has influential input in helping other ministries. Walker, like most pastors of great churches has a blend of many spiritual gifts. His father, Paul H. Walker was also an ordained minister in the denomination.

Paul Walker is first and foremost a preacher, and has built his church on his preaching. He is also a counselor, psychologist and educator; and no one will deny that he is also an outstanding business administrator. The $10 million dollar budget attests to that skill.

In the early days when the church was near the Georgia Tech

campus, Paul Walker felt that he needed more education. He
enrolled in Georgia State University (another large university in
the area) and completed a Ph.D in Psychology/Counseling. He
confessed that for many years, he was "counseling oriented" in his
preaching. This is another way of saying he preached to the needs
of people.

Over the years Dr. Walker's style of preaching has changed. He
says he is now more biblically based, meaning he is more exegeti-
cal. He also says, "I'm not as intellectual in my orientation as I
used to be, but this doesn't mean that I have abandoned my education. It just means that I communicate the Bible to people at
their level of need." He says he wants to preach passionately in a
way that touches the heart, while not ignoring the needs of the
mind. "I am more middle of the road in my preaching," he says.

Spirit-filled Worship

When asked about the reasons for the church's success, Walker
said, "We became the hub of charismatic outreach in North Atlanta
in the '70s." By this he indicated that his primary appeal was not
narrowed to a particular pentecostal audience. He saw a vast
number of people in mainline denominational churches who lived
empty lives, and he felt he could reach them with a heartwarming
message. He used contemporary themes, yet based his message
on the Bible. He used contemporary musicians, yet did not deny
the basic biblical ministry of music. "People in historic denominations were looking for a Spirit-filled ministry, and we became the
receiving church in North Atlanta for them."

The glue that holds Mount Paran Church of God together is its
worship. Walker says, "The church rises and falls on its Sunday
worship experience. We do not jump up and down in worship.
Yet we allow the expression of the charismatic gifts." The church
service begins with praise time, with the pastor becoming the
facilitator of praise and worship. Walker defines worship as the

total expression of the heart to God in adoration and praise. It is not secondary, nor is it achieved with mere "atmosphere." Rather, worship is, in Walker's words, the "high water mark" of the believer's experience, the highest point in the week of a person's expression to God. He therefore feels an obligation to plan quality, expect quality and deliver quality in the Sunday worship.

Mount Paran was large enough for people to enjoy a quality platform ministry, yet, the size allowed people anonymity so they could be lost in the crowd. To meet this need, the church was organized by small groups and multiple ministries so that no one was overlooked who came looking for help. Walker notes, "People came for the 'touch of God'—an experience—not for doctrine."

As in most southern churches, the Sunday School at Mount Paran became larger than the worship service over the years. But when this trend reversed, with worship attendance outgrowing Sunday School, Mount Paran also became a leader in developing an exemplary platform ministry. (The "tip point," or halfway point between the two movements, was reached in 1971.) "We depended on Sunday School for growth for many years," Walker said, "but that is no longer the case. Now Sunday School follows the worship and does not give it leadership."

Program and Organization

Walker realizes that "Programs can chew up people." By this he means that church members can become so busy keeping programs going that they cannot minister to the Body. The church does not have an organized outreach program as do many southern churches. They do not go door-to-door visiting, nor do they have an aggressive outreach to prospective new members. The church grows by relationships, and by word-of-mouth witnessing by people who find they get something from the service when they attend. When people hear what God has done for their friends at Mount Paran, they want the same experience.

Mount Paran does have an organized follow-up program, however. People who visit the church are contacted by phone and a letter within three weeks, or earlier when they request a visit

---

Don't fear failure. Fear of failure "kills innovation more than any other cancer."

---

from one of the pastors. When a new member joins, they go through membership training to get the whole picture of the church. They are assigned a Sunday School class and a Vine Life group. The purpose is to get them into some form of ministry and networked with other believers. The church uses Evangelism Explosion techniques to train people how to win their friends and others to Christ in a uniquely developed Mount Paran program called Personal Witness Training.

Mount Paran has never gone into the busing ministry. But it has a number of specialized ministries such as the Christian Rock Band, for young people, and the School for Ministry Development, a two-year program designed to help people find their ministry (last year 65 graduated). There is Vine Life, a program of small groups designed to keep contact with the 10,000 members. The Metropolitan Bible Studies began in members' homes to teach people the Word of God. Other programs are Alcoholic Victorious groups, Homosexual Anonymous and other counseling groups for people with addiction problems; and a ministry to children of divorced parents.

Walker says Mount Paran is not a Boomer church, but is equally divided among all ages. They tend to use traditional music, rather than innovative Christian rock music. He finds their music appeals to all ages of adults.

Strategy for Innovation

When asked how he has successfully begun so many different ministries, Walker listed an eight-point strategy:

1. *New ministries must be built on the longevity of the pastor.* People have to trust leadership before they follow leadership.
2. *A leader must share his vision of a new ministry, and the people must buy into the vision.*
3. *A leader must develop a reputation for integrity.* People must be able to believe what the leader is saying, before they will follow him.
4. *Always try to test a new program, before implementing it churchwide.* "I do this and find that way, I am not locked into a new program that may not work. Usually the church tries a program for three to six months before going public or making a permanent commitment."
5. *Get a few people to buy into a new ministry, but recognize that not everyone will buy into it.* One of the secrets of Dr. Walker's success is realizing that not everyone in his church will become involved in every ministry, and not everyone will be at the church building every day.
6. *Give everyone a loophole.* This means giving everyone the opportunity not to take part in a program, without feeling guilty. "Guilt," Walker says, "is an accusatory sense of failure. It is one of the diseases that kills spirituality and hinders programs.

    "By giving people a loophole, they can accept the existence of a program without feeling obliged to get involved or attend. When people do not feel an obligation to a new program they will not attack it or try to kill new ideas. But if they are not given a loophole they will feel guilty and intimidated and will try to kill the new ministry."

7. *Don't fear failure.* Fear of failure, Walker believes, "kills innovation more than any other cancer."

8. *Never be afraid to try something, but at the same time be willing to recognize when it is not working.* "I drank at that cup and learned valuable lessons."

The Impact of Prayer

When asked for the greatest answers to prayer in the life of Mount Paran, Walker readily named four:

"The *first* greatest answer to prayer is people."

"The *second* greatest answer to prayer in the life of Mount Paran has been the healing miracles," he said. And he delivered to this author a stack of over 100 written testimonies of people who said they had been healed at the church.

"The *third* greatest answer to prayer has been God's raising up of people to minister where needed," Walker said. This includes both full-time and lay ministries.

"The *fourth* greatest answer to prayer was the provision of finances." Walker then gave two examples of God's provision of finances in answer to prayer:

When the church first began televising in the '60s, they used black-and-white equipment. The television ministry, "Courage for Christian Living Series," had a tremendous response from those who had been helped. But they were stymied by limited equipment. In answer to prayer, one man sold his yacht to provide finances for a studio, equipment and outreach for the program.

And when the church first moved to Mount Paran Road in 1966, they needed $10,000 desperately. After doing all he could do to get it, Dr. Walker by faith committed the need to God. He says that God then awakened a man in the middle of the night, who phoned Dr. Walker, and by noon the next day the church had the $10,000 they needed for the project.

The Horizon

Walker feels that the church must become more mobilized to actively train people for service. His goal is to quickly establish and mobilize 500 Vine Life groups. This will help every person in the church become involved in ministry. Second, he wants to strengthen the platform of the church for worship, music and preaching, planning to reach people through the worship and mature them through Vine Life. And in the third place, he wants to liquidate the church's debt. Walker likes to pay cash for everything, and the church would like to do more for missions and to plant new, indigenous churches.

As Walker notes, the church's future is as solid as the foundation on which it is built.

ANALYSIS:
Elements of Innovation
for Today's Churches

11
NEW EXPECTATIONS: WHEN THE BOOMERS TAKE OVER

TRYING TO PREDICT WHAT THE CHURCH OF THE FUTURE WILL BE LIKE IS as simple as reading fortune cookies, yet it is more than merely guessing what will happen in the years ahead. Valid indicators can guide us. Just as we can find clues to the future personality of a girl by looking at her personality when she was a baby, we can find clues of the development of the future Church by examining the personalities of those who will be its leaders.

The leaders of the Church within the next 10 years will be those between the ages of 25 and 45—the Baby Boomers. By the turn of the century, the American Church will be a Boomer church. This does not mean that all churches will have a rock band to lead worship, or readings from *The Living Bible*, nor will worshipers necessarily attend church in Izod pullovers or sing only praise choruses. But to understand the Church of the future we must understand the values, objectives and life-style of today's Boomers.

Baby Boomers are the kids that were born between 1946 to

1964. They have been characterized as "the Pepsi generation," "the Now Age," "the Me generation"—along with a number of other phrases that describe their preoccupation with themselves. As Boomers marry, their self-indulgence extends to their marriage or family, and they are characterized as the "We generation."

In the business world, Boomers will take over middle-management positions within 10 years. They will become heads of corporations, senior members of law firms and members of boards of directors. Of more importance to us, they will be sitting on church boards and running our churches. They will be the senior pastors of the large churches that will influence and give direction to the rest of the church. Our need to understand them is obvious, since their life-styles, values and objectives in life will become a major influence in the Church of the future.

A Nation Ruled by Its Young

The Boomer culture is different from other historical adolescent subcultures because it has endured past the teen years. In past generations, kids ultimately have conformed to the values of adults, and the values of older members of society have thus been perpetuated. But not this time. Now, American adults searching for the eternal fountain of youth are worshiping at the Boomer shrine. These adults now tend to conform to the younger generation, rather than the reverse.

Boomers have a different view of life than their parents. Inasmuch as people are a product of both their homes and their culture in addition to the genetic and physiological contribution of their parents, Boomers are different because they were raised in a world that is unlike any other previous period.

Their parents were products of the Great Depression, the greatest corporate failure of America. This tended to make their parents realists, and, in some cases, pessimists. But the Boomers have never experienced such widespread economic failure.

We may have failed in the Korean or Vietnam wars, but this did not impact the life-style of the younger generation like the Great Depression. As a result, Boomers are optimistic and positive. Everything is "a-go-go." Boomers are winners.

Four Reasons Boomers Are Different

Boomers grew up in a world of four unique "causes" that never existed until their generation: (1) The Pill and birth control; (2) the atomic bomb, and the threat of instant and total annihilation; (3) television as the ubiquitous baby-sitter; and (4) Dr. Spock, with his

---

A staggering 233,452 babies were born nine months after V-J Day. This great Baby Boom is the source of the word "Boomers."

---

positive reinforcement child-rearing methods. Just as every cause produces an effect, so Boomers are the product of what was thought to be the perfect world for which their parents fought World War II.

During that war, the birth rate dropped to one of the lowest times of recordable productivity in the history of the United States. Our males were off fighting a war, and the female population was mobilized to keep industry running at home. However, in the year immediately after World War II, 3.4 million live births occurred, the highest number of babies born in United States history. A staggering 233,452 were born nine months after V-J Day. This great Baby Boom is the source of the word "Boomers."

All of the scientific technology that helped American industry

provide the basis for warfare became available for peacetime productivity. Work hours became shorter, work places became safer,
work effort became easier. Hence there was a change in the American attitude toward work—a change in the work ethic.

With work becoming easier, the Boomer attitude toward work
is different from that of their parents. They may work as hard as
any previous generation, but the values they bring to their work is
different. They do not necessarily produce a different amount of
work than their parents did, but their attitude and their expectations of the form and function of work are different.

The Sexual Revolution

Every generation has lived with sexual temptation, sexual promis-
cuity and sexual abuse. In modern times, however, sexual restraint
has been released like a burst dam, and its impact on the Boomers
is apparent. Having access to the Pill gave the Boomers sexual
freedom never experienced by other generations.

Sexual freedom is another way of saying they had "safe sex"—
safe, at least, from the penalties of unwanted pregnancy. Before
this, young people had some limited access to birth control methods and other forms of protection; but the Pill gave 24-hour protection, anywhere, anytime, on any occasion.

All this made a profound impact on sexual mores among
Boomers. Sex was now available for "fun," not just procreation.
Also, the Pill took away the possible stigma of pregnancy out of
wedlock. And it put the couple in charge of sexual results, rather
than being controlled by the natural physiological laws built into
the body.

As a result, Boomers developed a new attitude toward sex.
First, since that which had been reserved for the bedroom was no
longer a threat, it became acceptable on television. Next it became
enjoyable to talk about and to portray in the media. Finally, that
which had been risky or prohibited became the norm of life.

Growing out of the Boomers' new sexual awareness came the bikini, the miniskirt, adult-only movies, *Playboy*-type magazines—in essence, a sexual revolution. Side effects of the revolution have included more working wives, the changing and interchanging of sexual roles between man and woman, a more tolerant view of homosexuality, and so on.

The Positive Generation

Dr. Spock's book, *Dr. Spock Talks with Mothers—Growth and Guidance*, helped to form a permissive generation of children who were not corrected for doing wrong but only encouraged to do right. They grew up in a permissive atmosphere without the previous restraint. "Spare the rod and spoil the child" was no longer the norm of child-rearing. Boomers had a number of positive role models on television, in programs such as "Leave It to Beaver" and "My Three Sons."

This is not a criticism of the emphasizing the positive in child training and education, but an effort to point out the need for balance. Two truths about education should be apparent. First, negative correction teaches a person what not to do, while positive exhortation teaches them what to do. Dr. Spock created a "yes" generation by positive motivation, but the end result tends to lack the negative influence that usually produces character in an individual.

With the absence of guilt in the Boomers, plus their open attitude toward sex, we see a generation that appears outwardly to be happy, flirty, effervescent and always smiling. Whether this is what they are or what they want to be, it is surely the image portrayed in media. Many people older than the Boomers have difficulty with this. Most of them were Depression babies, having been reared in a period of national failure. While not necessarily pessimistic, they are more aware of failure and would probably call themselves "more realistic" in their orientation.

On Being a Boomer

The Boomers became a subculture with an unsatisfiable thirst for conformity. Boomers want to wear the same clothes as other Boomers, talk the same way, listen to the same music and drive the same kind of car. In this they are not unlike former generations where peer pressure drove the teenage subculture to conformity; yet Boomers seem to have carried their adolescent subculture into young adulthood. They are still an identifiable group that is dissimilar to other generations and other groups around them.

What does this say for a life-style separate from the world, that conversion to Christ requires? Many Boomers want the advantage of Christian values, but they don't want to be considered odd, weird or dissimilar from their contemporaries. They want to be "in."

In light of these changes, what do we see when we view a typical Sunday morning worship service? We see people who are positive, clean, neatly dressed, healthy and wearing that effervescent smile. Is this not the dream of Christianity? In essence, a Boomer personifies what many seek in Christianity.

Yet there is another side to Boomers that hardly fits the image of the ideal Christian. Whereas, during the '60s, the failure rate for marriage was 25 percent (one out of four), Boomers have doubled that rate with a 48 percent divorce rate (one out of two). And even though Boomers are outwardly positive, they are the generation of mental depression, anxiety and stress. Never before have there been so many counselors, psychiatrists, and mental health technicians.

Within the Boomer subculture is a smaller group called the "yuppies"—young urban professionals—who comprise a distinct class. These are the successors of the "yippies"—members of the '60s Youth International Party—who revolted against society, demanded freedom from restrictive norms, rejected wealth and status, and moved into communes. The yippies were also called "flower children," because some yippie antiwar protestors placed flowers in the rifle barrels of National Guardsmen. Some suggest that yippies were "postmaterialistic" in their value systems.

Researchers for politicians originally saw in yuppies a distinctive political and social attitude that separated them from the rest of society. They were under the age of 40, lived in urban areas,

---

Many Boomers want the advantage of Christian values, but they don't want to be considered odd, weird or dissimilar from their contemporaries. They want to be "in."

---

considered themselves professionals and were highly success-oriented and therefore upwardly mobile. Yuppies were well educated, well off and considered more liberal in life-style than the rest of the population, yet more conservative on economic and political issues.

A cover story in *Newsweek* magazine proclaimed 1984 "The Year of the Yuppie," primarily because of the strong showing of Gary Hart in the presidential primaries. Hart represented a yuppie mentality to media.

For all the attention given to them, however, there are not that many of them. Some researchers feel that when the field is narrowed to those who have a college education or professional employment, and who earn at least $35,000 a year, yuppies are limited to a very small percentage of the population—estimates run from 1 percent to 3.4 percent. However large or small their numbers, yuppies have the potential to form our opinions because they are moving into places of leadership and management where they will make decisions about the thinking, buying patterns and attitudes of Americans.

Three questions define a yuppie.

- *First, what is young?*
  Generally, the ages of 18 to 39.

- *Second, what is an urban dweller?*
  Someone who lives in a town of 100,000 or more.

- *Third, what is a professional?*
  Someone working in a job classified as professional
    by the United
  States Bureau of the Census. Not everyone who calls
    himself professional, in fact, fits the bureau's defini-
    tion.

What is known about yuppies? They are more likely to be Democrats than Republicans, yet they are conservative (some call them "neo-conservatives"). Their conservative bent, however, is not holistic.

They are more likely to support the legalization of marijuana, to recognize homosexuality as legitimate, to support atheists who want religion out of the public schools and to oppose the military establishment. Yet they are conservative in that they tend to reject higher taxes, government regulations, social spending and the New Deal agenda. They want laws providing greater sexual and gender freedom and equal rights for women, and they reject narrow sexual views in general.

Boomers in the World of Work

More deserves to be said about the work attitudes of the Boomer generation. America was built on a Protestant or Puritan work ethic which implies, among other things, the virtue of hard work.

This ethic is not true of Boomers, who are likely to criticize their parents for being "workaholics"—people who work because "it's there" or because it's self-fulfilling. As we said, Boomers work hard, but for different reasons. To the Boomers, work must have function and form.

Boomers will not be tied to work for the sake of work, nor to a goal for the sake of a goal. Their fathers worked by the axiom, "Do whatever it takes to get the job done." For Boomers, quality is the key word. Their axiom is, "A job worth doing is worth doing well."

Recently a seminar speaker likened church work to digging a hole. The foreman tells workers to go dig a hole, saying, "There's a lot of dirt to be moved, and you could help by moving dirt anywhere you see it." So workmen take shovels and begin digging a hole. They don't know how wide or how deep to dig it or even where the hole should be dug. They dig for the sake of digging—for the sake of the hole.

Ministry is often portrayed in the same manner. A young Boomer pastor is hired as an associate to a senior pastor. When asked for a job description, the senior pastor smiles and says, "Just find your niche, work hard and glorify God." He wants the young pastor to go out and win souls and visit the sick—like digging a hole, the work of God is everywhere, and without end.

Whereas the senior pastor works for the sake of work, this idea turns the Boomer off. He wants a job description and a job production scale. He wants answers to the questions: What must I do? and How much must I accomplish?

When a 34-year-old Boomer heard the analogy about digging the hole, he said, "Tell me how wide, how deep and exactly where you want the hole. And come back tomorrow and the hole will be there." He went on to say, "Also, I won't use a shovel. I want the best tools. I'll use a backhoe."

In the old days, people worked hard even when it was unpleasant and distasteful. Perhaps they were influenced by the biblical stigma expressed in the curse in the Garden of Eden: man should work "by the sweat of his brow" (see Gen. 3:19). Whereas the older generation often thought of work as essential but distasteful, the Boomers see work as fulfilling and affirming.

They don't mind hard work, just like they love to play hard. They work hard at exercising, at jogging and at their occupation. They work hard at anything that is fulfilling, but they don't sweat just for the sake of sweating.

What is meant when we say that Boomers are concerned about form as well as function? In the old days their fathers worked in the factory among steel shavings and oily floors, eating their lunch out of a pail while sitting on some boxes. This setting does not satisfy Boomers. They not only want job performance objectives (function); they want a clean work place and a positive environment (form). They don't mind working hard, but they want to enjoy the process.

At work or play, the fathers of Boomers would wear an old shirt that was no longer fit for Sunday dress. They had one pair of sneakers for every activity. Not so with the Boomers. They must have appropriate clothing, appropriate shoes and the appropriate tools, since form is just as important as productivity.

In the world of recreation, they must have jogging shoes, walking shoes, shoes for racquetball, as well as shoes for tennis, golf and bicycling. The shoe is just as important as their productivity. One Boomer said, "It doesn't make any difference how well you do what you do; it is how well you look when you do what you do."

Form also includes the tools of the trade. Boomers are perfectionistic; they want to work with perfect tools to accomplish a perfect job. They will not use a flat-headed screwdriver in place of a Phillips, nor a handsaw in place of a power saw.

Whether the latest toy to help work become simpler is a computer, calculator, mobile telephone, dictaphone or voice-activated computer, having the proper tools is essential. The secretary who is trained on a computer word processor will not take a job where she has to use an IBM Selectric typewriter, even if the IBM is the top of the line.

Boomers are not pro-company or pro-organization. Although they are generally loyal, their higher loyalty is to themselves. After all, they are the "Me generation." While they can be motivated to accomplish great things for the company, they do not respond well to goals set by the company or the boss. They respond to goals they have helped set and to purposes they have helped shape.

Boomers are the personification of the corporate management team. They want to work for a company that is managed by a team approach or by shared leadership. Three phrases describe the Boomer executive: (1) shared goal-setting, (2) shared problem-solving and (3) shared decision-making. When you see Boomers working on a business problem or a television commercial, it is always with a group.

Their fathers were the bosses who made decisions by themselves, alone in their office. Conference rooms were places where only the board of directors met. Today there is a conference room, even for secretaries, to plan strategy or work out problems.

Boomers and the Church

What does all this about Boomer attitudes say about the work of the local church? When Boomers get in control, they want the latest tools and technology. The old Sunday School record book will be replaced by the computer spread sheet.

The general adult class of the past will be replaced with age- and need-graded adult classes, taught with a variety of teaching aids that plug into the wall. The general door-to-door visitation strategy will be replaced by technology-oriented programs such as the GRADE program of the Wesleyan Church, Evangelism Explosion or the F.R.A.N.Gelism (reaching Friends, Relatives, Associates

and Neighbors) program of the Church Growth Institute in Lynchburg, Virginia—programs that can train lay leaders and match
them with reachable prospects.

Boomer attitudes necessarily carry over into church settings.
Boomers are often criticized for being more loyal to themselves
than to the Church. They will do what is best for them, not necessarily what is the best for the larger Body.

Boomers do not attend church on Sunday night because they
are supposed to; if they attend it is because they believe church
has something for them or will improve their life-style. Nor do
Boomers come to prayer meeting simply because it is the thing to
do. They are not as loyal as their parents to church attendance in
general. If they attend, it is because they perceive that it has a
function in their lives.

Just as Boomers reject control over their personal life from
their work or society in general, so they reject control from the
Church. They want to be involved in the decision-making process
and will not generally attend a church that makes decisions for
them. They want input in the decisions affecting their lives. They
will not support a church where goals are set for them, problems
are solved for them or rules are made for them.

Because they prefer to direct their own destiny, they will
attend the church that is "people motivated" rather than "pulpit
controlled." Boomers will not work in Vacation Bible School simply because there is a need; they will work when they receive
something for the time they spend. A key phrase to understanding
the Boomer is that "they want value in return for their investment
of time, energy or money."

Boomers will not attend a church where second-rate ministry
in second-rate buildings is carried on by ill-prepared leaders.
Boomers have always had the best. They have had the best baby-
sitters—television, the best clothes, the best school facilities; now
they want the affordable best church ministry without compromis-
ing their personal standards.

They will not attend churches where the pastors ramble, the music is shoddy and the facilities are rundown. In the old days their parents lived by the motto, "We will make any sacrifice for God," and they would applaud musicians who were sincere and did their best. Boomers see that as a cop-out for second-rate ministry.

Sincerity and desire are not enough. They will not settle for less than the affordable best. They want better than their parents had, and they want it now.

Churches tend to be conservative and traditional, but not Boomers. Although, as we have seen, they are conservative in some areas but they also tend to be antitraditional. They will not tithe simply because Christians are supposed to tithe or because it's the Christian tradition. And they will be turned off by high-pressure appeals for money, rejecting motivation by guilt or tradition. They will tithe when they get value in return for money expended.

Because of their overall conservatism, however, many Boomers will be attracted to the Church since it is often society's preserver of values. They may not like the "church of our fathers," but they will like the church of Jesus Christ.

The Age of Dysfunctionalism

Dysfunctionalism, an emerging factor in modern life, means that a person does not respond adequately, normally or as expected to the demands of living. Boomers are generally dysfunctional in sociological and psychological motivation.

Past generations experienced life like a stream of water that ran behind their houses. The stream could be analyzed at any place, and the chemical analysis would be the same. So our fathers had the same texture of life from day to day, changing only gradually as the demands of life slowly changed.

But Boomers are dysfunctional in the stream of life. Modern

life is changing too rapidly to analyze it consistently at different points. Life is no longer like a stream of water behind the house, but like several different kinds of pools behind the duplex—the swimming pool, spa, hot tub and wading pool. Each body of water is a distinct module of experience, with different textures and purposes.

Modern life is changing too rapidly to grab any handles. Boomers are the product of television, that has both reflected their life-styles and created new ones. Within a three-minute segment of commercials, they may be exposed to Coca-Cola, hemorrhoid medicine, floor wax and designer jeans. Each commercial jerks them from one "pool" to another, exposing them to new sense experiences and new stimuli to which they must respond. In a single series of commercials they experience guilt, laughter, grief and comedy—all within 90 seconds. The result is that the Boomer has had to learn to turn off and block out experiences, and to adjust emotions rapidly from one set of feelings to another.

This stress produces a dysfunction that tempers all of life for the Boomers. When they turn to a Bible teacher they can continue to adjust to or accept the experiences to which they are exposed without any discontinuity of conviction and/or eruptions of religious response.

The young people of the '60s felt that the traditional structures of society were meeting neither their needs nor the needs of society. Therefore they marched, burned, demonstrated and flaunted their freedom. Woodstock was a symbolic rebellion against America's past.

But Boomers are different. Yuppies are not yippies. Where yippies bailed out, yuppies have joined the establishment to change it. They still believe that old structures are not healing the ills of society, so they are going to throw over the old and create the new.

Some have asked if the yuppies will be "pioneers" or "settlers." Obviously, they will pioneer new institutions and create new relationships. They will reject rigid, authoritarian ministers. They will sit on church boards and want to be heard.

And more than being heard, they will make a difference. They will fight empty traditionalism. If they can't win, they will not submit; they will go to another church.

Basically, Boomers will want to use different tools to do ministry in the future. With their concern about form and function, they will want to reach their own generation, with their own tools and in their own way.

Boomers will accept biblical objectives and biblical principles. They will submit to Jesus Christ and will serve in His Church. They will change their parents' church into their church.

But the question remains: Was the past church *His* church, and will the future church be His church?

12
NEW WORSHIP STYLES: THE FOCUS IS THE SAME

The Priorities in Choice

Historical

Historically, when Protestants moved they usually chose a new local church on the basis of doctrine, not on the basis of worship style. While the style of worship was important, doctrine was the final criteria. The priorities were (1) doctrine, (2) name, and (3) denomination.

Most denominations had a characteristic style of worship that went with people's denominational or doctrinal loyalty. Presbyterians tended to choose a Presbyterian church when they moved, and if one was not available they would choose a church with Reformed theology. But even stretched to the limits, Presbyterians would probably not have chosen a church with Pentecostal or Arminian beliefs. One would have expected them to choose a church that at least held a similar view of eternal security.

Denominational alignment meant people were comfortable with a church's heritage, life-style or policies. In the past, most

> ## How People Historically Have Chosen a Church
>
> 1. Doctrine
> 2. Name
> 3. Denomination

denominations were not influenced by interdenominational television services and by ministers trained in interdenominational seminaries. Because denominations were relatively homogeneous, people could transfer from one church to another and fit in rather comfortably because there was little difference from one congregation to another.

Americans generally have not been quick to choose a church with a nonstandardized or nontraditional name. People have chosen churches with names that tended to be acceptable as "mainline" names—Methodist, Presbyterian, Baptist, Episcopal or Lutheran. Everyone knew what these names reflected. Nonacceptable names were generally Holiness, Temple, Pentecostal, Nazarene, Mennonite or a Bible church. To mainliners these names represented a sect, an unknown entity or an outcast group.

Contemporary
Today, Americans are not so picky about church names. Now they choose a church primarily by its style of worship or its philosophy of ministry. People are not looking for denominational labels, doctrine or a predetermined name. Presbyterians are no longer looking for a church that is covenant in doctrine or Presbyterian in name.

They may attend and join a charismatic renewal church because they enjoy clapping, lifting their hands or singing praise choruses. If they feel comfortable, they feel this is the way God should be worshiped. So they sublimate their doctrinal preferences and abandon their tradition for a new philosophy of worship.

What is the primary source of this change? It is coming from without the Church, not within. Culture is influencing the Church more than the Church is influencing culture.

What is in our culture that is influencing the way Americans choose churches? It seems to be no single thing but the whole thrust of society—the thrust toward consumerism.

Culture is influencing the Church more than the Church is influencing culture.

Americans consume everything from groceries to clothing to furniture to cars to entertainment. Consumerism is evident in television commercials, newspaper ads and the public relations segment of the business world. Consumerism is the engine that drives American society, and it is the driving force guiding them as they choose their churches.

Before the Industrial Revolution of the 1840s, America was an agricultural society, with 92 percent of Americans living and working on the farm. With the Industrial Revolution, people moved to the cities, and American culture evolved from a rural society into an urban industrial society to provide jobs and income. The nation became one of the world's largest producers of steel, cars and machinery.

After World War II, America changed again. We were no longer a producing society, but a consumer society. Now the glue that holds our culture together is buying and selling.

Less than 25 percent of our society is employed to produce something. Less than 5 percent work on a farm.

We are a nation that is driven by consuming things. The majority of our people work as salesmen, service technicians, consultants, managers, waiters, and so on. We sell to one another, serve one another and live off the profits of a consuming society.

Our favorite pastime seems to be walking the malls, not necessarily to buy something but just to shop. What we call shopping is really "consumering." We buy what is comfortable, enjoyable, flattering or entertaining. In the same way, America's Protestants choose churches on the basis of what affirms us, entertains us, satisfies us or makes us feel good about God and ourselves. And, to a growing degree this freedom of choice is also the the reason some Roman Catholics and others from non-Christian religions switch to Protestant churches.

If we recognize church worshipers as consumers, we will recognize church programs as menus, and types of worship as the main entrees in the restaurant. Consumers need food to keep them healthy or to keep them from starving. But, in a nation with lots of food, consumers go where the menu fits their taste. Americans can pick from fast food, Chinese, Mexican, fried chicken, a steak or from an abundance of other options.

A similar variety of consumer options is available when it comes to churches. The church menus Americans seek are not filled with doctrinal options but with a variety of worship options. Americans go where they feel comfortable with the style of worship that best reflects their inclinations and temperament:

A Lutheran couple chooses a charismatic renewal church because they like positive exaltation. Perhaps they thought their former Lutheran church was dead.

An independent Baptist leaves his revivalistic service to attend a Bible expositional church because he feels his former church was superficial and the new church has in-depth teaching.

A Pentecostal leaves the church of his birth claiming that "wild fire" has no place in his life. He chooses a liturgical worship experience in a Lutheran or Episcopal church where the formal liturgy enables him to stand in awe of the majesty of God.

The Salvation Army sergeant major leaves the familiar sur-

How People Currently Choose a Church

1. Function: the style of worship
2. Form: the quality of ministry
3. Doctrine: belief that influences life-style

---

roundings of the citadel to become involved in the small groups of a Body-life-type church. When someone tells him the sermons are not holiness-oriented as in the Salvation Army, he doesn't care; he is affirmed by his new-found relationships.

No matter what the style of worship, there seems to be a two-way door in and out of most sanctuaries. New people are entering to seek its strength, while others are tired of the routine and leave to seek their Sunday morning "high" elsewhere.

So the old phrase "the church of your choice" no longer means your doctrinal choice. Like buying a sweater, "the church of your choice" is a church that reflects your style of life and your way of worshiping God.

While these motives are negative factors in our churches because they minimize the doctrines taught in the Word of God, there is one plus. More nonchurch people are coming to our churches than ever before. When people come to churches where they are affirmed or where their life's goals are supported, consumerism has resulted in an open door for evangelism.

Styles of Worship and Ministry

Historically, there have been two basic worship styles in the Protestant Church since the Reformation—"high church" and "low church." To describe them functionally we might refer to them as the liturgical worship service and the informal style of worship.

Liturgical worship usually follows a printed order of events that include the Doxology, the Lord's Prayer, choir anthems, responsive reading of Scripture, choral response to the pastoral prayer, the Gloria Patri and the singing of "Amen" at the end of each hymn. Many believe the formal liturgical church service is a carryover from the Roman Catholic Church—the Reformation changed doctrine but didn't change the style of worship.

The second type of worship has been the expression of the common people in church groups that did not come out of the main stream of the Reformation, that is, the Brethren of the Common Life, Anabaptists, Moravians and others. After the Reformation this second worship tradition would be carried on by such groups as the Methodists, Baptists, Mennonites and Brethren.

These groups were usually led by pastors without professional education who preached extemporaneously without a written manuscript. The preaching was emotional, persuasive and filled with illustrations and the idiomatic language of the common people. "Sweaty preaching" by "plowboy preachers" called for revival and renewal—and, in response, there were tears at the mourners bench. The singing was carried on with expressive emotion. The services included testimonies, prayers from laymen and, in some groups, shouts of "Amen" or "Hallelujah!"

Defined by worship styles, six types of churches can now be identified within the Protestant Church: (1) the evangelistic church that focuses on winning the lost; (2) the Bible-expositional church that emphasizes teaching the Word of God; (3) the charismatic renewal church that focuses on expressing the miraculous gifts of the Spirit; (4) the Body-life church focusing on fellowship (*koinonia*), relationships and small groups; (5) the traditional liturgical church, which is still operational; and (6) the informal church of the common people, also still operational.

Six distinct philosophies of ministries and church growth have

---

Six Worship Styles

1. The evangelistic church
2. The Bible expositional church
3. The charismatic renewal church
4. The Body-life church
5. The liturgical church
6. The informal church of the people

---

emerged to match the six styles of worship on the American scene. At the center of each style of worship are several catalysts or types of "glue" that hold the church together. Whereas most protestant churches will do many of the same things in worship or ministry—pray, sing, collect money, preach and so on—the *way* these things are done and the value that worshipers give to them make them distinctive. Each ministry style adds a unique value to one's experience of worship, making it different and, to many, desirable.

The Evangelistic Church
The term "evangelistic" describes a style of ministry that emphasizes such activities as door-to-door visitation for evangelism, the altar call, Sunday School busing, and personal evangelism. These ministries, often called "soul-winning," are prized among an evangelistic church's members.

One example of such a church is Bill Hybels' Willow Creek Community Church of South Barrington, Illinois (while Hybels disagrees with my assessment, I cannot place his style of church in the other categories). Hybels calls his Sunday morning service a "seeker service" where the unsaved can feel comfortable, barriers to their salvation are removed and sermon topics are titled to appeal to them.

We can find evangelistic-type churches among Presbyterians, Congregational, Pentecostal, Baptist and other denominations. The doctrine of a denomination is not the determining factor that makes them evangelistic.

An evangelistic church usually (1) is action-oriented, as opposed to meditative or instructive; (2) has strong pastor leadership; (3) has persuasive evangelistic preaching to get people converted; (4) has simplistic organization; (5) is organized to get lay people involved in outreach; (6) is growth-oriented (numbers-oriented); and (7) is platform-oriented. Usually, the success of the platform ministry of preaching, special music and the evangelistic appeal will determine the success of the church.

The Bible Expositional Church

This church is usually noted for its use of sermon notes, overhead projectors for people to follow sermon outlines, expository sermons, reference Bibles—such as the *Ryrie* or *Scofield Reference Bible*; and constant references to the original languages of the Bible. The dominant spiritual gift of the pastor is teaching. At almost any given service the congregation can be seen taking notes and keeping the pastor-teacher's presentations in a notebook.

This church usually appeals to the upper-middle class and will be found in a college or white-collar community. A true Bible expositional church is rarely successful in a blue-collar or redneck community. This type of worship crosses denominational lines and can be found in Baptist, Presbyterian, Methodist, Independent Bible or a variety of other groups.

The pastor probably learned his preaching style at Dallas Theological Seminary, Talbot Theological Seminary, or some other independent seminary—not from the denominational seminary.

He might have learned it from some interdenominational organization such as the Navigators or Campus Crusade for Christ.

The Charismatic Renewal Church

This church is usually described by its feeling and flow. Worshipers feel free to lift their hands in worship or clap them in joy. They sing praise choruses, go to the altar to pray, hug one another and laugh or cry.

They lay hands on one another for healing, power or anointing. Most of the charismatic renewal churches exercise the miracu-

---

Like buying a sweater, "the church of your choice" is a church that reflects your style of life and your way of worshiping God.

---

lous gifts of tongues, healing, "word of knowledge," "slain in the spirit," interpretation or other expressions of the Holy Spirit.

Not all charismatic renewal churches are oriented to the Pentecostal style or miraculous gifts, however. I have talked to several Southern Baptist pastors who were being pressured by their local association because of the renewal style in their worship services, not because of the exercise of miraculous gifts. Sometimes the pressure came from the fact that these churches dropped adult Sunday School and extended the worship service from 10:00 A.M. to noon.

The pastors told me they had not changed their doctrine, They were Baptist, supported the cooperative program and didn't believe in the miraculous gifts. But their worship style was irritating to the local Southern Baptist Association.

Charismatic renewal churches can be found among Presbyterians, Episcopals, Roman Catholic, Pentecostal and the rapidly emerging independent churches. Theology is not the dividing line, hence doctrine is not the glue that holds them together. They may preach "power theology," "prosperity theology," Pentecostalism or old-fashioned liberalism.

The emphasis in these churches is on personal renewal in fellowship with God. A person can speak in tongues as a prayer language, without the Pentecostal second blessing. This style of worship is not found in the formal services of a liturgical church, but in the intense experience of pouring out personal love for God.

Whereas formal liturgy emphasizes that "the Father seeketh such to worship him" (John 4:23), worship in a charismatic renewal church focuses on two-way communication between the person and God. The worshipers must get something out of worship. It must be stimulating, uplifting and exhilarating. They like worship, and it affirms them. When they go home, they feel good about what they have done.

The Body-life Church
The glue that holds this church together is the relationships that are formed in the small groups or cells that make up the Body. It is in the small groups that pastoral care happens and people grow spiritually. A Body-life church has a lot of hugging going on and places value on transparency—being open and honest and caring in their groups. They confess their faults to one another, are accountable to one another and pray for one another.

Body-life churches do the other things that normal churches do, such as preach, sing, teach and worship God. But they prize highly the quality of life they receive from relationships. In a given session they might testify, share burdens, pray for a hurting brother and share a blessing or an answer to prayer. It is "the Body ministering to the Body."

A Body-life church is not a pulpit-dominated church where everyone looks to the pastor for ministry. Instead, a Body-life church congregation looks to one another for support, help and ministry. It focuses on *koinonia* or fellowship within the Body.

Just as in the other cases, Body-life churches are found in Baptist, Evangelical Free, Independent or Pentecostal churches. The influence of *koinonia* crosses denominational lines. It is not a church style that is taught in most seminaries, however. Pastors learn it from one another, from conferences, from seminars or as they intern under a body-life-style pastor.

The Liturgical Church

The traditional formality of this worship style was described earlier in this chapter. In some churches, the style of worship has not changed since the denomination's founding, and people sing the same hymns that were sung by their grandparents. While some feel a liturgical service is dead, others feel invigorated because they know they are obeying God who "seeketh such to worship Him."

Liturgical worshipers do not worship for a feeling. They center all glory, praise and worship on God. He is the focus of the worship service. The people are not there to evangelize, to learn, to fellowship or to be renewed. Worship is obedience to God.

The Informal Church of the People

This is the church where the people want preaching that reflects who they are and speaks to them. They want sermons that are devotional, yet also include some teaching, motivation, renewal and worship. The pastor is a shepherd who is one of them and has arisen from them. It is a "low church," in that authority is with the people, rather than being a "high church," with authority situated at denominational headquarters away from the people.

I used to call this a Baptist church, because the people were responsible for the entire life of the church—they are self-governing, self-propagating and self-supporting. But all six worship styles can be "Baptist" in this sense, with the people more responsible for the church than the pastor or the denomination, doing the work of ministry in Sunday School, training programs, camps, VBS and the like. One of the main gifts of the pastor is to organize the people for ministry, rather than doing ministry for them.

Why Now?

These six styles of worship or philosophies of ministries seem to have come to the surface in the past two decades. They were not apparent in Victorian England, colonial America or even before World War II. Until the influence of American Christianity spread abroad, these six church styles were not evident in churches or groups of churches outside our borders. While all six qualities have been embryonic in every true church since Pentecost, it seems now that certain churches are characterized by a dominant trait or style, and that this strength has become the catalyst around which the people gather. So why have these dominant worship types manifested themselves now in certain churches and in certain new denominations?

The answer lies in the impact of two explosive forces that have shaped our society in the past 40 years. These two formative factors have done to culture in general what they have done to the churches—shaped them into six groups. These two factors are (1) the interstate freeway and (2) the computerized television screen.

The interstate highway system is a massive transportation link that joined the two coasts of America and made the shopping mall available to anyone within 25 to 50 miles. These concrete networks crisscross every state, making almost every destination available to everyone.

So now people will travel as far to church as they travel to employment or to shop. They travel 30 miles to church and never think of the distance, because church is only 30 minutes away. Whereas, the colonial farmer may have traveled one hour by wagon to get to a church that was geographically many miles closer.

The computerized television screen stands for modern communication. People have access to almost any fact in our information processing age. Churches tell their story on cable television and local radio, in church newspapers and metro newspapers, on billboards and by various other inventive means. Everyone seems to know about the various kinds of worship we have been describing, because they see people worshiping like this on television. Then they decide to drive 30 miles to experience it firsthand. They like what they experience and come back every Sunday.

A retired man and woman drive 150 miles every Sunday to my church. I asked them why they come so far. The wife said, "When you get over 70 and nothing else in life matters, why not go as far as you have to if it's a church you like, and your church is the high point of the week?"

Obviously, they don't come back for Sunday evening services or Wednesday prayer meetings. But their reasoning is hard to refute. Why *not* do what you enjoy in life?

Spiritual Motives

Some spiritual factors are behind the emergence of these six worship and ministry styles. In the past three decades we have witnessed an explosion of interest in spiritual gifts. At first the curiosity was about tongues: Do you or don't you speak in tongues?

While tongues don't seem to be as decisive now as they were in the '70s, the interest in spiritual gifts is still with us. The present drive to study gifts comes from the average Christian who wants to know "What is my gift?" and "How can I serve God with my gift?"

Each of these six styles of worship have a dominant manifestation of a different serving gift. This means that a specific spiritual gift holds the worship and ministry together. The Bible expositional church is driven by the spiritual gift of teaching. The obvious spiritual gift in the evangelistic church is the gift of evangelism.

Gift Colonization

In fact, these six styles tend to be colonies of like-gifted people—a situation that has been called "gift colonization." People with an embryonic gift choose a church where their personal dominant gift is also the dominant corporate gift. That's why they feel comfortable in a particular style of worship. They are around people like themselves. This is not a selfish desire to avoid people who are different, or who may make them feel uncomfortable. People just naturally sort themselves out in life by arranging to spend time with those who make them feel good and help them accomplish their goals.

True, the church is a hospital where sinners came for help. But the church is also an island among the terrifying tides of life, a haven where believers can escape for safety and solitude. Churches turn out to be different from each other because of this "gift colonization." The average Christian knows this because of the computerized television screen; and he is able to attend the church that emphasizes his own gifts because of the interstate.

Gift Gravitation

The process may also be called "gift gravitation." The driving force for Christians to find a church is probably not within their awareness. They don't know why they choose a charismatic renewal or a liturgical church. They just know what they like. The need to exercise their own spiritual gift creates pressure—a kind of internal disequilibrium, driving them toward the church where their gift is honored and exercised by others, and where they are appreciated for exercising their gift.

Gift Assimilation

The final factor explaining the current emergence of the six types of churches is "gift assimilation." Christians like a church worship style, but may not be able to explain why.

Comparison of Gifts with Worship Types

Worship Type	*Dominant Spiritual Gift*
1. Evangelistic	Evangelism and prophecy
2. Bible expositional	Teaching
3. Charismatic renewal	Exhortation (positive and practical)
4. Body-life	Mercy-showing
5. Liturgical	Helps (serving)
6. Informal	Shepherding

Using the evangelistic church as an illustration, people enjoy what they see at the church altar. They are affirmed when people get saved. As they band around soul-winners they get a burden or desire to win souls. They might have thought they didn't have the gift of evangelism, but as they share their faith with lost people they find their gift of evangelism growing.

The Bible teaches that a person can grow in a spiritual gift: "Eagerly desire the greater gifts" (1 Cor. 12:31). The more new members are around others with the gift of evangelism, the more that gift grows. "Gift assimilation" is another explanation for the variety of "gift colonization."

Clarification

The observation of six different worship and ministry styles is obviously general in application. All churches have some manifestation of gifts, and probably no one church has just one practicing spiritual gift. Most probably have two or three, and our own viewpoint determines the one we see.

These six types can't be applied too broadly to all denominations. For example, while we may find all six types among Southern Baptist churches, most of these churches tend to be type six—the low church or the informal church of the people. Their strength is their people.

Christians in a style of church that fits their spiritual gift will probably sublimate their theology to the worship practice. This doesn't mean they minimize doctrine, it just means the commands of Scripture to worship take priority over their perception of doctrine. And since doctrine is theoretical, they give priority to worship, which is outward and functional.

After all, worship is an observable, measurable, repeatable action that can be compared to other churches. One's belief or a belief in doctrine is not observable, measurable or repeatable. It's hard to compare the life-style resulting from a belief in dispensationalism with that arising from a belief in covenant theology.

Since the six worship styles are based on six spiritual gifts, all of them are biblical, which means all are correct. The other side of that truth is that none of them is wrong or unbiblical. As you examine the churches of this book, realize that they are all biblical churches, although they express different styles of worship.

Since in their church services they all have a biblical expression of worship, those who criticize them need to learn more tolerance. They need to realize that God accepts different worship styles, as long as they are biblical. Also, those who think their style is the "right" style or the only style should think again. Tolerance is a necessary tonic for all bigots.

But there is another observation for those with an obviously dominant worship style. It's the word *balance*. The evangelistic church needs the balance of strong Bible teaching, fellowship and worship. Each church in this book could learn something from the others who do worship differently.

As a matter of fact, I have found the 10 pastors in this book to be broad in their understanding and acceptance of others. Their strength is in being able to appreciate others while remaining committed to their own dominant gift and style. Since, "God uses people where they are usable," these pastors are effective because they emphasize their own giftedness without the intolerance that maintains that their way is the only way.

May God continue to bless them for their perspective that obedience in worship of our heavenly Father through Christ can be done in many different ways.

13

THE NEW ROLE OF PASTORAL LEADER-SHIP: FROM MINISTER TO EQUIPPER

D R. W. A. CRISWELL, PASTOR OF FIRST BAPTIST CHURCH IN DALLAS, was listed in my previous book, *The Ten Largest Sunday Schools and What Makes Them Grow* (1969). Criswell was then president of the Southern Baptist Convention as well as pastor of the largest Southern Baptist church in America, which at that time was a church of 6,000 people in attendance and 20,000 members.

Dr. Criswell said he was intrigued with my examination of the role of pastoral leadership in the great churches. I had pointed out that the largest churches were built by pastors who had long tenure, who were dynamic leaders and who led their churches to grow. Conversely, I wrote that the great, growing churches were not "committee bound," nor were they board-dominated.

Dr. Criswell told me, "I've always agreed with your observation that great pastors build great churches, average pastors build average churches and weak pastors lead weak churches." He said that pastors who exercised biblical leadership with the people could lead a church to grow.

"Churches that are dominated by deacons have a difficult time growing," he added. And he concluded that "the pastor is a shepherd who leads, the deacons are those who serve and the people are the final seat of authority."

Some rejected my observation in that book that growing churches had strong pastoral leadership. They wrongly thought I meant dictatorship. I do not believe it is biblical for a pastor to be a dictator, but it is biblical for pastors to lead a congregation.

What's wrong with dictatorial pastors? Even though some dictators cause growth, that doesn't justify their actions. Some dictatorial pastors have done what they wanted with money, resources, bond issues, salaries and so on.

Some people have been run out of their church by dictatorial pastors. Some pastors split churches because of greed, power or ignorance. No one needs dictatorial pastors because they harm churches, they harm believers and they harm the testimony of Christ.

The new churches have a new role for pastors. We need pastors who will lead churches in soul-winning, not become the only soul winner in the flock. We need pastors who will lead churches in ministry, not become the only one serving God. They need to lead in stewardship, prayer and vision. Everyone in the church needs to be in Bible study, service and discipleship, and the pastor must lead the congregation in these areas.

We do not need more platform churches where everything is measured by the pastor's ministry. A platform church is where the pastor is primarily the Bible conference teacher or the evangelist or the catalyst for worship. A platform church is where the engine that drives the church is the pulpit and the congregation is along for the ride.

The New Testament church focuses on pastor and people. The

pastor leads the people so that all members use their spiritual gift in a ministry within the church. The Bible teaches that every member should have his or her ministry. We are to grow up in Christ, from whom "the whole body, joined and held together by every supporting ligament, grows and builds itself up in love, as each part does its work" (Eph. 4:16).

The New Testament church focuses on pastor and people. The pastor leads the people so that all members use their spiritual gift in a ministry within the church.

A Baptist pastor in Virginia insisted that all new members joining his church go through a membership class and, during that experience, take a spiritual gift test to determine their spiritual abilities. They were then given an explanation of places of ministry in the church and the leadership training necessary to serve with each position. As these new people signed the application for church membership, they signed up for service.

When the new prospect was introduced to the church for congregational vote into membership, the pastor told the congregation what their dominant spiritual gift was and where they would be serving. It was a case of "if you have no ministry in this church, you have no membership."

The pastor sends two powerful messages to his flock with this announcement and requirement. First, it is expected that everyone who sits in the pew also have a ministry; and second, their church is not a platform church.

Biblical pastoral leadership requires a ministering group of people who follow the pastor. There is a reciprocity between leadership and fellowship. If a dictatorial pastor is not biblical, then a congregation that allows their shepherd to run over them or minister for them is not biblical.

The opposite of that situation is also true. A congregation or board that wrestles pastoral leadership from the pastor is not biblical, nor is the pastor who rolls over to their demands. Just as a balance of authority between the executive, judicial and legislative powers makes a strong United States, so a balance of authority makes for a strong biblical church.

There are many descriptions of leadership, but I use the following two-point definition:

> First, leadership is *influence.*
>
> Second, leadership is *plural.*

Leadership Is Influence

Stating the opposite, that leadership is not control, gives insight into the first point of the definition that leadership is influence." As a matter of fact, the more a pastor tries to control a church, the less likely it is to grow. Small churches can be controlled; large churches cannot be controlled.

Many pastors think they must control people or events to make the church grow. They control the budget, the election process or the decisions. They are comfortable with control and uncomfortable when they don't get their way. But leadership is influence, not control.

Why is control wrong? Because the church belongs to Christ, not to the pastor. Christ is to control the church's money, decisions and people. He communicates His control through every member—the priesthood of the believer—by:

• His indwelling presence in every believer;

- The access every believer has to the Scriptures, to read and to interpret them;
- The responsibility members have to cleanse the church of apostasy and sins of the flesh. See the instructions Paul gives to the members of the congregation in Corinth (1 Cor. 5); and
- Every member using his or her spiritual gift (1 Cor 7:7).

Almost everything a pastor does influences his people, so almost everything he is relates to his leadership in the church.

When a pastor controls his people he takes away their initiative to serve Christ, hence their opportunity to grow in Christ. He stifles creativity, growth and spontaneity. He needs to unleash the church, not control the church.

What is control? I know a church where the pastor owned the church building and when people voted by a majority to take away some of his freedom to control financial decisions, he threw a fit. The majority then voted him out as pastor.

He responded by yelling, "Get out of my building!"

Unfortunately, he made it stick. He kept the building and kept the church going with a remnant. The majority left. To make the illustration ridiculous, this is the same pastor who refused to supply me with statistics for a chart of the 100 largest Sunday Schools. He said it was unscriptural to emphasize numbers.

Leadership is influence. The more people a pastor influences, the greater his leadership. When I first got out of seminary I told a pastor friend, Wes Hunt, "I don't want to be famous, I want to be influential." At the time, I didn't know I was asking to be a leader.

The pastor influences by his sermons. He influences the growth of his people and what they think. He influences by his counseling ministry and decisions. He influences by his ability to solve problems and motivate people. Almost everything a pastor does influences his people, so almost everything he is relates to his leadership in the church.

Leadership Is Plural

The second aspect of leadership cannot be separated from the first: Leadership is influence *and* leadership is plural. We can never look at a leader in isolation. A leader must relate to those who are led.

The pastor must relate to his people. The shepherd must relate to the sheep. The one has little or no existence without the other.

To say that leadership is plural means that leadership is not what you do *to* people; it is what you do *with* people. Leadership is a lonely job. But the leader is never alone.

Pastoral leadership means you are in front of the congregation, sometimes as a pioneer, other times as a guide. In the army, they call it "walking point." It is the most dangerous position in combat because you are the first to get shot at. Walking point means that leaders stand in front of the church so they can take the flack intended for the church.

Of course it's natural when you walk point to expect that the people behind you are supportive. Unfortunately, sometimes the pastor finds that the congregation has abandoned him. The pastor walks point but the people are not following.

What should he do? Should he criticize their support or lack of it? Should he call them names, such as "coward" or "unspiritual?"

No.

If the people are not following, it is a mark against the pastor's leadership. The pastor who constantly criticizes his people because they won't get involved in the church, needs to refocus his perspective. He doesn't have a congregational problem, he has a leadership problem.

If the pastor "outwalks" his people so they are not following, it usually shows lack of leadership ability on his part. Good leadership inspires followership. If the congregation rebels at all the pastor's ideas and programs, again it shows lack of leadership skills.

In the same way, we don't have financial crises in our churches. Every crisis, including a money crisis, is a leadership crisis.

Of course if leadership is plural, the pastor has less trouble when few follow. But the old Chinese proverb is still true: "He who thinketh he leadeth, but has no followers, is just taking a walk."

14

NEW INFRASTRUCTURE: FROM INEFFICIENCY TO A MANAGEMENT TEAM

THE CHURCH OF THE FUTURE WILL OPERATE LIKE A BUSINESS. THAT REVolutionary statement scares me, because while churches should be business*like*, they should not *be* a business. Some churches operate as a ministry, with operating procedures that are different from the world, and other churches operate as a ministry that is run like a business.

I see coming in the future a church that is all business. More than just operating as a business, it will be a business that is operated for souls. The Church will value image, marketing, cost-fund accounting, job description and institutional goal-setting.

In the early '70s, I talked about "Selling Jesus like we sell Coca-Cola." Some pastors violently objected to my statement. They felt that Jesus should be presented only in the context of the New Testament Church. They felt that prayer, preaching and worship was all that was needed to communicate salvation to the lost.

Back then, I disagreed with their limited view of evangelism. I felt they were overly critical of saying we could sell Jesus as we sell Coca-Cola. I felt that since God had given us radio and television to reach the masses, we should use more kinds of media and more exposure to present Jesus to the world.

Jerry Falwell gave credibility to this statement when he said, "I can reach more people in one Sunday morning telecast than the apostle Paul reached in a lifetime of ministry."

Since then the Church has not only learned to sell Jesus as it sells Coca-Cola, it has gone the second mile. It has gone into the business of selling Jesus, whereas, in the past, the Church only used the techniques of business to further its aims of world evangelism.

Now I am scared by what I see happening and what I believe is coming in the next decade. Already in many places I see the Church as a business. The Church is not just using business methods; the Church is becoming a business as a direct reflection of our business-oriented culture.

The Church as Business

The Church can use the same methods as businesses because many of the methods never originally belonged to business or to the Church. Certain principles are universal truths, and true principles can be applied both to the Church and to business. Truth should transcend both culture and history.

As an illustration, the truth of efficient principles applies to all institutions: the family, the school, the government, the Church, as well as businesses. When the Church learned how to use certain techniques that made its ministry more efficient, it was not a business just because business also used those techniques. *Being* a business is entirely different from the Church's becoming efficient in the business of ministry. But now some churches are beginning to step across the line: they are becoming a business that is also efficient in ministry.

Business is measured by the bottom line—profits. Good businesses make a profit, some immediately, others eventually—at least that is what the modern business person thinks. Profits are synonymous with modern business. Apparently, the days are gone when the business man who owned his shop was motivated by service to his customers and all he wanted in return was to make a decent living. He didn't have to show a profit to be successful, nor was his business driven by the bottom line.

If God has truly called the church to feed the poor, then it may be worth any sacrifice necessary to keep it going.

The bottom line has become one factor that makes churches into businesses. Church growth authorities assume that a church must grow in several areas, that is, money, converts, attendance, baptisms and membership or enrollment. Though church growth in itself is not wrong, the wrong expressions of church growth weaken a church.

The phrase "maintenance ministry" is used negatively to describe nongrowth churches. If a person is a maintenance pastor, he is not as well respected as a church growth pastor.

The church has blindly adapted the methods of business without evaluating them. This does not mean that a method can be sanctified by prayer or fasting. A method does not become biblical just because it is used to preach the gospel.

Business methods grow out of business objectives and make business the unique animal it has become. Before the Church uses a business method, it should evaluate the method carefully, lest it push the Church to focus on a business objective. In such cases, the church is suddenly a unique business animal.

One illustration is using "cost-fund accounting" to evaluate a church program. A secular business will assess all expenses to a department such as building use, insurance, postage, personnel, and so on. It can determine what areas of the business are out-of-line in expenses or what department is not showing a profit. Since profits are the bottom line, if a department cannot contribute to profits it is chopped, programs are slashed, factories closed and people fired. They may have been loyal employees, but they are history, nevertheless.

Cost-fund accounting can be brutal when used to assess the effectiveness of a program in the church. If the feeding program of the poor cannot attract financial support, it is killed. The problem is that if God has truly called the church to feed the poor, then it may be worth any sacrifice necessary to keep it going.

Suppose a church board votes to terminate a program. Did they make a mistake in originally beginning it? Or did they sin by killing it?

Did those who quit supporting it with their money make a mistake? Perhaps the blame lies with those who ran the program. Did they administer it properly to get enough support, so that they bear some responsibility for its failure?

This approach is a two-edged sword. Cost-fund accounting can save an entire ministry by locating a financial leak in an organization. Or cost-fund accounting can be a brutal instrument to change a church from a ministry-oriented institution to a business.

When the Church is controlled by the methods of business, it is on the dangerous edge. The Church as business will win souls, care for the sick and carry out other aspects of ministry. Efficiency of ministry or breadth of ministry are not the bottom line of a church. They are means to an end.

A particular local church can actually win more souls than any other church in its state and be walking on dangerously thin ice. How? In its efficiency, it is forced to cut out a program and release faithful workers. Their families and friends are crushed.

The unsaved see a Christian ministry release its own and think, *There is no difference between a secular business and a Christ-cen-*

tered ministry. The unsaved have a right to ask, "Would Christ fire faithful employees?" Can a New Testament church suddenly collapse a ministry on the basis of "cost-fund accounting?"

There are other abuses of the "church as business" toward its employees. They can be put in intolerable working conditions, not be allowed normal freedoms and be embarrassed or harassed, all in the name of efficiency.

The glue that holds a church together is different from business glue. Christ is the glue that holds a church together.

A business—or a church operated as a business—may use severe restriction and/or discipline to accomplish "company policy," but the employees do not willingly or joyfully comply. They are coerced. Even though the "church as business" policy says, "This is for the glory of Christ," or "This is to make Him known," when Christ is not the glue that holds the ministry together, when He is not the motivation of each worker, something has been lost.

The Church as Business and Ministry

There is a point of balance between the Church as ministry and the Church as business. On the one hand is the extreme of a church that just cares about people and almost ignores its business processes. It can't pay its bills and goes out of existence. On the other hand is the extreme of the business church where the staff operates 40 hours a week and clocks out at 5 P.M. in the face of need, just as surely as union workers punch the time clock when it's time to go home.

The point of balance is achieved in the ministry that is run as efficiently as a business, but it is not a business. The bottom line is not money, profits or a balanced budget. The bottom line is quality service to people, whatever it takes.

Ministry is not compromised and people's needs are not ignored. As a matter of fact, good organization can help a church reach more people and reach them effectively. Good organization honors God and is what God expects of a church.

Though the bottom line of a business is profits, an objective toward which the whole organization is directed, the business itself is held together by the glue of its organization. And business glue has many expressions:

• *Good job descriptions hold business together.* People make the business prosper when they know their job and how to accomplish it. So the personnel director constantly works at his job, which is to keep all positions harmoniously working toward the business goal.

Job descriptions explain: *What I must do.*

• *Job objectives are a second glue in business.* Sometimes called "management by objectives," job objectives hold a business together as each person works toward his or her assigned goals. The objective may be to install fuel pumps on a machine, or it may be to reach a financial goal in a division of an insurance agency.

Job objectives define: *What must I accomplish.*

The glue that holds a church together is different from business glue. While a church may employ job descriptions and job objectives, members of a church have a higher calling or a different motivation. While businesses use extrinsic motivation (profits) or intrinsic motivation (job description and job objectives) to generate and maintain employee loyalty, the church has a deeper motivation.

That motivation is Christocentric motivation. The church member serves to please a Person—Jesus Christ—who indwells him, helps him and ultimately will reward him. Christ is the glue that holds a church together.

Whereas a church may use job descriptions, objectives and even cost-fund accounting policies, Christ is everything. To say that Christ is everything is more than sloppy mysticism. Christ is the outward objective, Christ is the inner motivation, Christ is the standard of excellence and Christ (not profits) is the ultimate reward.

The Christian liberal arts college I attended has a motto, "To know Christ and make Him known." That is the kind of glue that sets a church apart from a business.

But hasn't the Church always been different from a business? Haven't church workers always worked harder, worked longer and made sacrifices? The pastor gets up in the middle of the night to comfort the parents of a child killed in an accident. The faithful Sunday School teacher spends extra hours visiting prospects.

The minister gives up sleep to rise early to intercede for his flock. These sacrifices are done for Christ and are motivated to please Christ. They are Christocentric areas of motivation.

The Bible teaches that the Church is both an organism and organization. As an organism the Church grows as a plant or as the physical body. An organism inherently grows, because it has life. The Church as an organism will grow because it has the life of Christ.

The Church is also an organization which is an outward expression with offices, job description, budgets and merit reviews. As an organization, the Church ought to be as well organized as IBM or Ford. The Church ought to be as well administered financially as any profit-making organization. The Church should never be sloppily run. It is not a good Christian testimony to be out-of-date or out-of-touch.

A pastor of a church on the north side of Atlanta ministered to upwardly mobile yuppies. The church met in an old concrete block building with a dirt parking lot. The pastor followed principles that were obviously obsolete.

The people of this Baptist church finally came to their pastor and told him, "We live in air conditioned homes that cost over $100,000, but our church is an old concrete block building with a dirt parking lot. We like the ministry, but we can't reach our friends through a run-down facility."

They went on to describe the ineffective organization. "We want to worship in a church that reflects our life-style," they said.

Making these changes would not necessarily make this church a business. If the motivation remains to reach people for Christ, operating more efficiently would help, not hinder, the church in maintaining its biblical witness.

15
NEW BONDING: FROM JOINING A CHURCH TO BUYING INTO A RELATIONSHIP

THE 10 CHURCHES IN THIS BOOK EXUDE EXCITEMENT IN THEIR SERVICES. When their members talk excitedly about their churches, the spiritual taste buds of those listening to them are tantalized because of the enthusiasm these churches generate in their flocks. The unchurched realize these churches have more to offer than most.

When outsiders visit these churches they, too, get all excited and plan to return again and again. If the distance is too far to return, they wish their church were more like the one they visited. Some even move their places of residence and get new jobs just so they can be part of a vibrant fellowship.

How do these churches create such enthusiasm in the unchurched? Certainly, the average church doesn't generate this kind of interest in nonmembers. Why?

Because the average church talks about church membership or

"joining our fellowship" as though it were speaking of joining the Lions Club or the Boy Scouts. The average church talks about church membership as though it were something a person has to do; it's described as an obligation.

But legalism never did excite the masses. And the contemporary world that does not understand loyalty and obligation does not respond to the normal emphasis on church membership.

The average church talks about "moving your letter" or "joining the church" or "extending the right hand of fellowship." These phrases apply to a person or family who has been converted and taught the obligation of attendance, tithing and participation. The average Christian family does this because they are expected to do so.

The Bonding Process

The old term is to "join" a church, or to be "assimilated" into a church fellowship. These terms were adequate when the average American was loyal to the institutions in his community. The new term is "bonding." When a person is bonded to a contemporary church, the process is similar to that when using Super Glue.

The old name for an adhesive was "paste" or "mucilage." It was just a gum or glue that stuck two things together. In the same way, church membership in the old days was the adhesive that held the member to the church, because it specified what a member must believe and how a member must behave.

Super Glue is not an adhesive. It does not *paste* two elements together, but *bonds* them, by absorbing itself into the elements of the two surfaces so that the two actually fuse or melt into one. In the old days, paste would break and things would separate. But when you secure two pieces of wood together with Super Glue, the wood will splinter before the Super Glue will break because the two are bonded into one.

Each of the 10 churches in this book bonds new people with

their church. The process is not mystical because it can be explained. But "bonding" is difficult for the untrained eye to see. Many visitors become loyal to the church before they officially join it. And new members are more loyal than those who were members before the present pastor came to the church. While each of the 10 churches bond with different methods or steps, similarities in contemporary culture make the nature of the bonding in each church similar to each other.

Three steps form the process of bonding a person to a church. They are: interfacing, buying and ownership.

- *Interfacing* means the person must face the church. This involves recognizing the church, relating to the church at points of communication and making an initial contact with the church.

  Later, new members will be involved in face-to-face interaction in a small group or cell where feelings are communicated—something that doesn't happen in the traditional class on church membership.

- *Buying,* the second step, is like a person walking into a store and buying an item or purchasing services. The concept of buying includes: (1) need, (2) desire, (3) knowledge, and (4) paying the price. We never buy something unless we pay the price.

- *Ownership* is the third step in bonding. The concept of buying implies transferring ownership from the seller to the purchaser. At this stage, an actual transfer of permission and authority takes place.

  When someone buys into a church, he or she not only has permission to be a member, but also has authority to be a member with all the rights and privileges of membership. Now that person feels it is no longer the pastor's church. It is "my church."

  When a new member gets "ownership" in a new

church, he assumes both responsibility for and accountability to that church. Of course, he is also accountable to
God. But when a person bonds to a new church, he must
gain ownership of excitement, ownership of worship
functions and ownership of doctrine.

New members must feel they possess the contagious
enthusiasm of the new congregation. And to get it, they
buy into the worship style.

Notice that "ownership of doctrine" (knowledge) is among
those concerns that are third in the above list. On a priority scale,
Americans generally feel that buying into doctrine is not as important as buying into "feelings" and "commitment." Therefore, in a
renewal/revival church a new member who is Calvinistic buys
into a church, even if it is Arminian in doctrine, because theology
has become third in his list of priorities.

Many times we feel that those who have been in the church for
a long time are the real owners of a church. They are the first class
citizens, and those who join later are second class citizens because
they do not have a history of what is going on. In the church of
the future, however, the bonding process will enable new members to know, feel and act in their ownership role in the church.

Bonding Cannot Be Forced

We should be careful not to use the word "bonding" in either a
mystical or a manipulative sense. Bonding is not something a
church does, but a relationship that exists between the new
believer and the local body. Bonding is something that happens as
a process of life. Just as people can be placed together but can't
be forced to love, so new members can be placed in a cell group
or Sunday School class but can't be forced to bond to a church.

Bonding Through Belonging to a Primary Group

Bonding means more than trying to keep a new member from dropping out of his new church. New members are best bonded to a new church when they belong to a primary group of the church. The primary group can be any smaller body of the church,

---

Bonding is more than teaching prospective members habits of church attendance or getting their tithe or correcting their behavior. Bonding is a total immersion into group fellowship, group values and group ministry.

---

such as a Sunday School class, a cell, the ushers, a ladies missionary group or the choir. It is more realistic to expect new members to identify with a small primary group than expecting them to identify with the total church or the larger group that worships on Sunday morning.

A "primary group" can be any group that a person identifies with. New members may not see themselves as an integral part of the large congregation, while a bonding can take place when they feel that, because they are a part of the process, a small group cannot function adequately without them. "Those ushers need me," a new member says as he considers not attending church.

When the new member projects himself into the small group in this way, it has become his "primary group" and his means of identifying with the church. A new member has bonded when she sings alto in the choir, sees herself as part of the worship process and feels the process would diminish without her presence. She experiences church ownership with a small primary group, an experience that couldn't happen with the larger group.

So bonding is more than teaching prospective members habits of church attendance or getting their tithe or correcting their behavior. Bonding is a total immersion into group fellowship, group values and group ministry.

When Bonding Takes Place

Bonding is often nonverbal and takes place when there is no official instruction of how to get into the new group. This means that bonding does not automatically happen when a person goes through a new membership class or is voted into the church.

Bonding can begin taking place before the sinner receives Christ because it is a part of the preconversion process. Also, bonding continues to take place after the act of receiving Christ and after the membership class is over, because bonding is also involved in the postconversion process. Although bonding is a process, it is most effective when it occurs simultaneously with conversion, as will be shown.

Bonding is similar to the process of "imprinting"—an act in the natural world whereby a newborn animal attaches itself, in a sense of belonging, to an agent that is responsive to it immediately after birth or hatching. A famous picture of the Nobel Prize winning naturalist Konrad Lorenz shows him being followed by ducklings. The ducklings attached themselves to him as the protective-parent.

As in ducklings, bonding produces a relationship that can withstand separations. The ducklings followed Lorenz everywhere and did not unlearn the relationship during periods of separation. It is as though God has placed in the newborn a divinely-engineered factor, whether psychological or physiological, that prepares them for bonding to a parent.

The process of imprinting animals after birth is similar to entrance into a new culture. It involves new sounds, new smells, new sights, new feelings and a new way of life. Studies show that the newborn is more alert during the first day after birth than at any time during the next two weeks. This implies there is an "alert time" to bond a newborn animal.

Bonding is similar to the process of "imprinting"—an act in the natural world whereby a newborn animal attaches itself...to an agent that is responsive to it immediately after birth or hatching.

By analogy, there is a proper time to bond a newborn Christian to a church. The phrase, "Win the winnable," takes on new significance, for it does not mean just winning them to Christ when conviction is strongest. It also implies bonding the new Christian into the local body immediately after conversion.

Animals or fowls will identify with surrogate or substitute parents, especially if the real mother is absent or has rejected them. Apparently, the state of being "lost" and being "found" in relational terms contributes to bonding. Our contemporary world of anonymity and "lostness" prepares people for the bonding process of these new churches.

Bonding, Conversion and Continuity

Some new Christians identify with a local church at conversion, and the relationship endures. Others go through a similar conversion experience, yet drop out of fellowship with the church and, apparently, with Christ. What are the variables that explain this difference among those who experience conversion?

1. Is the continuity experienced by some the result of regeneration? Are they truly saved, while others have only professed salvation?
2. Is continuity explained by adequate instruction of the new convert in the first steps of the faith, while those who drop out were not adequately instructed?
3. Is continuity explained by the level of "need fulfillment" offered by the new church?
4. Is continuity explained by the reputation, organizational or postconversion follow-up of the new church?
5. Is continuity explained by a strong bonding process when new members are incorporated into the fellowship of the new church?

Probably all of the above factors are involved in long-term commitment on the part of new members. Bonding, however, seems to make the greatest contribution to the continuity of a person professing salvation.

Timing Is Crucial to Bonding

Timing is crucial to bonding. New life appears to be born in a state of unique readiness, or as expressed previously, in an "alert time." This is another way of saying that there are "seasons of the soul." This timing seems to be emotional, psychological and physiological. Therefore, bonding occurs best when the participants are uniquely ready for the process.

The new Christian has gone through several experiences that prepare him for bonding:

- First, he has admitted that he is a sinner and cannot save himself. This admission usually involves a new self-evaluation that leads to a new self-perception and/or new self-awareness.
- Second, he has accepted Jesus as Savior, which, in many occasions, involves recognizing Christ as the Lord of his life. Again, this involves a new self-awareness.
- Third, there is usually a public confession that may involve baptism, testimony, walking down the aisle and the like.

These factors usually ready a new Christian for bonding in a local church. The radical absorption of self-perception into a new fellowship with God is pictured as a birth (John 3:3-7). The spiritual bonding to Jesus Christ that results in the believer becoming one with Him (John 15:1-5) is reflected in a social bonding to His local body; that is, spiritual baptism is reflected in water baptism.

Water baptism does not guarantee that a new Christian will continue with his new church, but it is one of the variables in bonding. Those churches that baptize new converts tend to have more continuity than those that do not.

The Law of Seven Touches
Studies show that new believers tend to drop out of the church if they do not become attached to a primary group within two weeks. This is illustrated when what I call the "Law of Seven Touches" is violated. This law indicates that when a church makes seven immediate and meaningful contacts with potential members and/or prospective converts, they tend to return to the church and convert or join the church's fellowship.

The Law of Seven Touches implies that a church must:

- immediately contact the prospect,
- be intentional in follow-up, and

- be systematic and varied in continual contacts.

Studies reveal that churches that make the most contact tend to do the best job in bonding new members to the church.

The Law of Three Hearings

Converts are more likely to bond after attending the church three or four times. This I have called The Law of Three Hearings. Therefore the church must use The Law of Seven Touches to get a prospect to return three times to get a possible bond of a new convert or a new member. Both laws are based on someone in the church establishing relationships with the candidate.

Even with intensive follow-up, however, some will not be bonded but will drop out of the church. There are several other reasons why some reject the bonding process. Sometimes "sociological clash" occurs. People of different cultures or different classes do not mix well While their love for Christ will motivate some to overcome cultural or class barriers, others cannot overcome them and drop out. Some drop out immediately, while others drop out after a period of time.

16

NEW POSITIONING: FROM SINGLE CAMPUS MINISTRY TO A MULTICAMPUS CHURCH

THE TRADITIONAL AMERICAN CHURCH IS USUALLY THOUGHT OF AS A small building on a small piece of property. Historically, people walked to church so no parking was needed, except in rural areas where farm families tied up their horses and wagons.

The traditional American church also had a sensitivity for the ministry of other churches, so much so that they usually respected the "turf" of another church.

The Extended Geographical Parish Church Defined

But with the emergence of an urban mindset and a "consumer approach to ministry," a new phenomenon has originated that I call "the extended geographical parish church." An extended geographical parish church is spread out over a larger area so that it:

- meets in several locations,
- operates different ministries in different locations, and
- has expanded its location geographically in order to reach a larger "Jerusalem."

Another way of describing this concept is:
- multiple ministries,
- multiple places of ministry,
- multiple ministers, but
- one central organization and one senior pastor.

Multiple Ministries, Multiple Places of Ministry

The New Pattern

The Perimeter Church of Atlanta, Georgia was intentionally planted at several locations along Interstate 275 on the north side of Atlanta in order to reach a broad sector of the metropolitan area for Christ. Two other churches in this book—Mount Paran Church of God and The Church On The Way—became extended geographical parish churches, but they did not begin that way.

By another definition, even a church that has cell groups meeting in homes over a vast part of their geographical area make a church an extended geographical parish church. In this book, such churches are reflected in Willow Creek Community Church, Central Community Church, Horizon Christian Fellowship and New Hope Community Church.

As we have seen, The Church On The Way in Van Nuys, California, expanded by leaps and bounds when it bought the facilities of the large First Baptist Church a quarter of a mile away and became an extended geographical parish ministry. In 1969, the First Baptist Church was listed as the eighth largest in America, with 2,847 average weekly attendance. The neighborhood was upper-class, white, sophisticated and located only a few miles from Hollywood.

But the neighborhood changed racially with poorer blacks, Mexican and some orientals moving in. Because First Baptist Church was committed to its upper-class-type ministry, it moved and followed its people 10 miles west. After The Church On The Way expanded to the former First Baptist facilities, it filled the 2,200 seat auditorium.

The new churches are therefore spilling out of their walls and off their main campus. They are expanding their ministry all over their "Jerusalem," hence expanding their geographical boundaries.

The Old Pattern

In contrast, most churches of the past were located in one area of the city, such as Highland Park Baptist Church or the Congregational Church downtown. This type of church drew from the entire city, but did not branch out with additional buildings into campuses around the city.

Multiple Ministers, But One Central Organization and One Senior Pastor

The New Pattern

Some churches in the next century will branch out for ministry's sake, yet will remain one church meeting in many locations for expanded ministry—meeting the definition of an extended geographical parish church. This is a multistaffed church, meeting in multilocations, offering multiministries, with a single identity, single organization, single purpose, single force of leadership, yet governed by the entire members from all parts.

Describing it negatively, no group can control another group, no group can pull out or splinter and retain its property, while individuals can resign at any time. These churches do not think of themselves as different parts, but as one body, one church, with one purpose and one nucleus.

Rev. Randy Pope began Perimeter Church with a vision of planting many congregations around the perimeter of Metro Atlanta, Georgia. Each congregation—the technical name for the smaller group—located in a different section of Atlanta was part of one church—the technical name for the composite group.

> *The new churches are expanding their ministry all over their "Jerusalem," hence expanding their geographical boundaries.*

After beginning eight congregations, Pope realized he couldn't reach his goal with the constraints of one church, so the several congregations reorganized into Perimeter Christian Ministries, Inc., which is a "transchurch" organization of eight local autonomous churches. The basis for their new eight-member fellowship is not Presbyterian Reformed doctrine, but their unusual forms and worship styles.

Each church will contribute 5 percent of its total income for the primary goal of planting other new churches of like practice. Obviously, they will be of like faith, too, but that's not the point. This new "denomination" is being formed on method, not theology.

The Old Pattern

In the past, large churches existed with "chapels" designed to reach various sections of the city. These chapels were defined as nonself-governing groups that depended on the mother church for strength and existence. When a "chapel" became strong enough, it became an independent church.

But the extended geographical parish churches are different in composition. No one section of the church dominates another or the whole, nor does one group hold the administration or the budget at the expense of the other. All members in each group are considered equal in status and influence.

Also, in the past there has been a "circuit" where one pastor was the minister for two or more churches. The Methodist circuit-riding preacher was an illustration of this form of ministry. This arrangement involved two or more autonomous churches separate from each other but joined by denominational allegiance.

Each church in the "circuit" system tended to be led by lay people, but ministry was supplied by the same part-time pastor who was paid a part-time salary. The extended geographical parish churches have the opposite infrastructure, being pastor-led rather then lay-led. Their emphasis is lay-ministry rather than pastoral ministry.

Each Church Its Own Denomination

Each section of the extended geographical parish church has local leadership (full- or part-time) to promote local ministry and local identity, yet retains a central system of shared management. The extended geographical parish church resembles a business with a main office and regional offices, rather than the traditional denominational structure.

The extended geographical parish church has been described as a small denomination or a minidenomination, because it is one local church, large enough and self-sufficient enough not to need the benefits offered by denominational headquarters. It can do everything for itself that headquarters would otherwise supply.

But the extended geographical parish church is different from a cluster of denominational churches or from an association of churches. It has a single government for all the parts (churches) and a single staff to promote a unified ministry, unified vision and unified identity. When one part of an extended geographical parish church ministers to unwed mothers or reaches a new subdivision, it is as though the whole church is operating through the one part. The permanent union of each part guarantees the continuity of ministry by each part, so that the total ministry is a joint venture of the whole church. It eliminates needless duplication of staff, programs and resources, such as one computer system, one accounting office and one maintenance office. Yet it can offer a wider variety of spiritual gifts, and it has a broader financial base to provide a stronger influence in ministry.

The Biblical Basis

The book of Acts seemingly provides a biblical base for the extended geographical parish church. The church at Jerusalem was one church (Acts 8:1), yet it was made up of several parts, or units. The Jerusalem church is described as a unit: "the multitude of those who believed were of one heart and soul" (Acts 4:32, *NKJV*). Note that the word "multitude" is singular; the church was one entity.

Yet later we are told that "believers were the more added to the Lord, multitudes, both men and women" (Acts 5:14, *KJV*). Here "multitudes" is plural, describing more than one entity. These were probably groups of classes or groups of people within the Jerusalem church.

The Jerusalem church was one large group (celebration), and many smaller groups (cells). The leaders went from house to house (Acts 2:46; 5:42, *NKJV*). This was probably not door-to-door soul-winning, nor was it "every member canvassing." Each cell of the Jerusalem church met in different houses for fellowship and ministry.

Apparently the early Jerusalem church did not serve communion in a large gathering or celebration, but served the Lord's table in small groups or cells that met in houses (Acts 2:46). Thus the large group in the Jerusalem church met for celebration, preaching, motivation and testimony (see Acts 3:11); and in small cells for fellowship, accountability, instruction and identity (see Acts 5:42). From these observations, I conclude that the norm for the New Testament church included both small cell groups and larger celebration groups.

The norm for the New Testament church included both small cell groups and larger celebration groups.

The traditional American church met in large groups (celebration) for the Sunday morning worship service. The function of small groups was carried out primarily in Sunday School. But the new emerging churches are meeting in small groups in weeknight flocks, Bible classes or care groups.

Different churches have different emphases in their small groups. Some, such as New Hope Community Church, emphasize fellowship. Willow Creek Community Church emphasizes Bible study, and Horizon Christian Fellowship emphasizes worship.

The church at Corinth also appeared to have several groups, as did the Jerusalem church, but these groups were wrongly divided. It appears that one group emphasized Paul, another Apollos and the self-proclaimed spiritual groups said they were of Christ (1 Cor. 1:12). Yet another group probably emphasized Peter (3:22).

Several smaller groups or house churches in Corinth contributed to the division. Instead of leadership bringing the Corinthian church together, they were also apparently divided by geographical and/or ethnic lines.

When Paul writes to the church at Rome from Corinth, he

reveals the make-up of the Corinthian church. He greets Priscilla and Aquilla and the church in their house (Rom. 16:4,5). He mentions "the churches of the Gentiles" (v. 4), which may have consisted of house churches or cells with predominantly Gentile members, meeting in the home of a Gentile—the homogeneous unit principle.

Paul also sends greetings from "the churches of Christ" in Rome (Rom. 16:16). The term "churches of Christ" is a descriptive phrase used to identify Jewish believers. The Greek term translated "Christ" was parallel to the Hebrew term "Messiah" or "Anointed One," the hope of the Jews. Hence the phrase "churches of Christ" may have been used to describe Jewish house churches—the homogeneous unity principle again—in Corinth.

Paul concludes the chapter with "the whole church saluteth you" (Rom. 16:23, *KJV*), a description of the total Corinthian church—the extended geographical parish church—of both Jewish and Gentile home-churches.

Summary and Conclusion

These early attempts to develop the extended geographical church nearly 2,000 years ago usually ended up with bishops over several churches. The mother church usually became a cathedral. In other ages the attempt ended up in denominational churches, each separate, but all united under one superstructure.

In other words, many have tried to build such churches, but with various results. It remains to be seen if those who are presently trying will succeed. The world is certainly different now, with changes that could never have happened three decades ago. Perhaps these changes will enable current experiments to succeed.

As we have seen, the present extended geographical parish churches are the product of two innovations—transportation and communication. Because we have telephones, computers, fax machines and all types of media to communicate a church's structure and goals, it's now possible to build a super church in many locations. Also, because we have interstate highways, cars and ease of travel, a megachurch can be located in several places, yet connected by efficient mobility. These churches are a product of our times.

The question remains: Are they a product of the New Testament?

17

NEW DENOMINATIONS: FROM THEOLOGY TO METHODOLOGY

IT SHOULD NOT SURPRISE US THAT THE NEW STYLES OF CHURCH DESCRIBED in this book have resulted in clusters or fellowships of like-minded churches that are, in effect, new denominations. But the churches involved in this trend are being brought together by different forces than those that attracted the formation of the old denominations.

The old denominations include "mainline" denominations, evangelical denominations and even those denominations formed within fundamentalism. The new denominations are not just those that have recent vintage. They are driven by a different engine, and must be viewed by different standards.

If the old mainline denominations are like Model T Fords, then the evangelical or fundamental denominations are like sleek Thunderbirds. And, although they are not the same car, they are still gasoline-driven automobiles. But the new denominations are like rocket-driven helicopters—a whole new mode of transportation.

The Glue That Binds

The Old Denominations

The main catalyst of the old denominations was doctrinal unique-ness—a group of churches joined in fellowship because of similar theology. A doctrinal statement represented the reason for a denomination's existence. Even churches that lacked an official doctrinal statement were at least connected by a similar hermeneutic, by a method of Scripture interpretation or by a like orientation to Christianity in general.

In some cases denominations have split over various aspects of theology, usually forming two new denominations. But the glue that held denominations together was primarily doctrinal in nature.

So, in the past, a person looking for a church made his choice on the basis of doctrine, denominational name or denominational alignment. It was important for a Presbyterian to choose a church that taught eternal security and covenant theology. A Pentecostal chose a church because of its position on "secondness"—sanctifi-cation as a second grace.

When people crossed denominational lines it was because they first had studied the belief of the new church. They wanted to be sure what doctrine was taught, whether it was biblical and whether it agreed with what they believed. It took an "act of heav-en" to move a Calvinist to join an Arminian-based church.

And when people jumped from one denomination to another they were rebaptized, attended a class or were interviewed about their beliefs by the pastor or church board. Often a pastor or Roman Catholic priest would refuse to marry an interfaith couple until the errant spouse joined his church.

Barriers were set up by both sides of a denominational argu-ment. In an attempt to make their people "good Baptists," many pastors were anti-Presbyterian in their teaching or rhetoric. Bap-tists and Presbyterians argued over the form of baptism, both claiming to be correct and biblical, and both denouncing the other side.

If the barriers were meant to keep their people in, they also kept out people from the other side. It was like erecting a six-foot chain-link fence to keep people in the "right" church fold, then stringing strands of barbed wire at the top for extra protection. Three strands leaned in to keep the sheep in, and three leaned out to keep the goats out.

The New Denominations

Formerly, a doctrinal statement represented the reason for a denomination's existence. Today, methodology is the glue that holds churches together. A statement of ministry defines them and their denominational existence.

And just as denominations split over doctrine in the past, new denominations are sometimes born now in a split over methodology. And illustrative of this phenomenon are the two denominations in existence today that have grown out of the ministries of Chuck Smith and John Wimber. Chuck Smith began his Calvary Chapel ministry in Costa Mesa, California in 1965. And Calvary Chapel proved so successful that many other similar churches soon began to spring up, first around Los Angeles and then outside California, but still primarily in the western states.

John Wimber worked with Chuck Smith in the Calvary Chapel movement in Southern California in the early '80s. Wimber had been attracted by the "soft" charismatic style of Calvary Chapel. The church had the freshness of new worship and praise choruses, Bible teaching and the credibility of godly living.

But Wimber was more committed to church growth by the "signs and wonders" movement, and he wanted more expression of miraculous gifts in the worship services. Smith, however, had come from a denomination that had vivid Pentecostal expressions such as "healing lines," and he did not want that manifested in his church. Yet both John Wimber and Chuck Smith believe in modern-day healing, tongues and miraculous gifts, and both are charismatic and holiness-oriented. They disagreed simply on the style of worship and expression.

They separated, and some churches left with Wimber, becoming part of the Vineyard Fellowship. Others remained with Smith within the Calvary Chapel fellowship of churches. Today there are two strong new "denominations," born out of differing methodologies and expressions of ministry.

The contemporary American wants the freedom to first be himself before God. He doesn't want to put on pretenses, especially in the light of a holy God who knows the sincerity of his heart.

Other emerging movements or embryonic denominations move onto the scene through pastoral conferences where their methodology is communicated to all who come to learn "how we did it." Dr. John MacArthur, pastor of Grace Community Church in Sun Valley, California, has a yearly pastors conference called the "Shepherds Conference." In this gathering he espouses, among other things, expositional preaching and elder leadership—a style I call the Bible expositional type of church (see chapter 12). MacArthur has a school to perpetuate this methodology—The Master's College—and an administrational attempt to give the movement direction through a new central organization called "The Master's Fellowship."

Jerry Falwell did the same thing in the late '70s, with his Super Conference for church leaders. His school originally was Lynchburg Baptist College, with the specific goal of training pastors for the movement. But it has become a Christian liberal arts university with goals that are broader than training pastors. Falwell also organized Liberty Baptist Fellowship to plant churches, and Liberty Baptist Mission to send missionaries to the foreign field.

Hard Center, Soft Edges

These emerging denominations tend to attract churches of similar outreach or worship styles. The principles taught in their conferences make up the catalyst for this attraction and also keep nonpracticing churches from "full fellowship." The hard core of these movements consists of, not doctrinal issues but, *the standards by which effective ministry is measured.*

The leaders of these emerging denominations and usually the leaders of the pastors conferences tend to be both totalitarian and biased against those who do not use their methods. Not only do they believe their method to be more functional than others; they usually denounce their rivals for methods they view as (you pick one!) unbiblical, out-of-date, apostate, nonworkable, nonanointed and so on. In their narrow commitment to their unique method, they usually present it as the best form of ministry, if not the only way to do it.

This narrowness of allegiance to method—normally reserved for a cult or sect mentality when associated with doctrine—is the energy source that drives the leaders to form these new denominations. They must organize a pastors conference for others, because they consider theirs the best and most efficient method, or because they view it as more biblical.

The new denominations will grow as a young baby when proper attention is given to it. Leaders sacrifice for ideas to which they have given birth. They get their greatest satisfaction from seeing their newly discovered methods grow up in other areas, just as parents take understandable pride in their children when they "make good" in the world.

Choosing a Denomination by Consumerism

The new denominations reflect the trend in consumerism that emphasizes function or style. The average American is seeking a church that expresses his desire to worship God. The church consumer doesn't want the church to mandate what he must believe.

He wants the church to provide services in which he can worship God, and teaching that imparts biblical values to his children and helps him live a better life. The contemporary American wants the freedom to first be himself before God. He doesn't want to put on pretenses, especially in the light of a holy God who knows the sincerity of his heart.

Comfort Zones Are Primary

The key word is *comfortable*. Modern Americans want to be comfortable in their worship and church style as much as in their lifestyle. This is not comfort for comfort's sake, as a person may wear a comfortable sweater because it feels good. The contemporary Christian wants the kind of "worship comfort" that flows from doing what is an honest expression of his heart and from engaging in that which is meaningful and affirming to him.

The new denominations are a catalyst of worship, evangelistic or nurturing styles of church. While doctrine is important to them, it seems to be secondary both as the glue that holds the churches together and as the attraction that draws the consumer. Like yuppies, the new denominations are a fellowship of churches who share similar "comfort zones" with others who are attracted to this or that unique style. Just as yuppies are comfortable dressing like other yuppies, with special clothes for jogging, aerobic classes, tennis and bicycling, consumer Christians are comfortable in churches with their style of worship or fellowship.

Doctrinal Differences Are Secondary

In the old days the nontongue-speakers "threw rocks" at the

tongue-speakers, just to scare them away and keep them from sneaking into their churches with private charismatic calls designed to proselyte the faithful. Those who spoke in tongues "threw rocks" at nontongue-speakers, invoking 1 Corinthians 14:18 and being quick to argue with anyone that they were like Paul: "I speak in tongues more than all of you."

The contemporary Christian wants the kind of "worship comfort" that flows from doing what is an honest expression of his heart and from engaging in that which is meaningful and affirming to him.

But the rock-throwing has subsided in recent years. Charismatics are not proselyting as much as in the past. Tongues are used more as a prayer language than as an overwhelming gift of the Spirit.

That manifestation of tongues-speaking doesn't intimidate nontongue-speakers as much as does the claim that tongues are an evidence of the baptism of the Spirit—the Pentecostal experience— that imparts over sin a spiritual power or victory that the nontongue-speaker doesn't have. Now the issue of tongues seems to be how they help one to function in his Christian life, rather than who is right or wrong. Tongues no longer seem to be tied to theological exclusiveness.

Just as doctrine is submerged by the consumer Christian and is not the primary catalyst for fellowship in new denominations, it may also have to ride in the backseat of the car in other areas of church life as some of the older denominations are compelled to consider or undertake mergers. Several denominational groups are struggling to keep their heads above water. They face a decline in membership, money, ministerial candidates and general vitality. When this setback happens, they often start shopping around for a like-minded group with which to merge. In 1969, the Evangelical United Brethren merged with the Methodist Church to form the United Methodist Church. While most of their doctrine came from the same general school of theology—holiness and Arminian—the differences that originally motivated pioneers to sacrifice for a separate denomination were sublimated for the merger.

The Pilgrim Holiness Church merged with other Methodists to form the Wesleyan Church, and now the Wesleyan denomination is discussing a merger with the Nazarene Church. The Lutheran Church of America merged with the American Lutheran Church. So just as new denominations are singing their doctrinal music more softly these days, similarly the older denominations seeking merger are now de-emphasizing certain doctrines once held inviolate.

"Like Ministry" Is Essential

Let's not be too hard on such groups. They are not erasing all doctrine off the chalkboard as a teacher erases yesterday's lesson. But they do not view doctrine "ontologically"—as their primary reason for existence. They are not grounding their ecclesiastical being in the definition of doctrine, nor on the claim that they alone are biblical or correct.

The emerging denominations see doctrine as a means to an end. That is, they see their doctrinal uniqueness as reflected in life or in their style of worship. They feel that being correct or biblical is not a matter of reducing doctrine to paper, but a matter of how we respond to God, whether by raising hands in worship or in an expositional sermon focusing intensely on the Word.

Therefore, both the catalyst for forming the new denominations and the impetus for merging old denominations usually falls within broad doctrinal parameters. Calvinists fellowship with other Calvinists, but they allow each other the freedom to dot the *i*'s differently *as long as the style is similar.* To illustrate, a group of Calvinistic churches will fellowship with other churches that have their expression of confrontational evangelism—busing, door-to-door visitation, altar calls and the like.

But Calvinism is not the key. These churches would break fellowship with each other quicker over styles of preaching or over whether an invitation is issued after the sermon, than they would over five-point or four-point Calvinism or other doctrinal issues that separated them in the past.

The new denominations do have a deep commitment to their doctrine when theology is expressed in worship. New allegiances grow out of unique expressions of worship or out of worship that finds its fulfillment or compatibility in doctrine. Differences in outward style often grow out of doctrine, and can cause a split in church fellowship that is as deep as the doctrinal splits of the past.

Other expressions of unique styles may result in new denominations in the future. Larry Lea, pastor of the Church on the Rock in Rockwall, Texas, centers on a unique type of prayer ministry. Other new denominational groups are expressions of prosperity theology, with television programs, conferences and pastoral training sessions.

Another current fact of church life is the presence within denominations of subgroups with a ministry purpose that is contrary to that of the larger group. Sometimes these smaller movements want to return the denomination to what they perceive as its original purpose, such as the Good News movement in the United Methodist Church. At other times the subgroup has organized itself with new objectives, such as the Southern Baptist Alliance movement within the Southern Baptist Convention—a group that is trying to organize a new seminary in Richmond, Virginia.

The growth of the new Bible colleges formed by the churches

of these emerging ministries is sometimes interpreted as "branching out on their own." The old Bible colleges, those formed prior to the 1950s, are fighting for their financial lives. Even though they have accreditation, buildings and tradition, they continue to struggle.

Some Bible colleges drop out of existence, some have marked decline in attendance, some merge. But few are as robust as the new Bible colleges supported by the emerging churches with newly discovered techniques and dreams of successful movements that will build churches, capture cities, win the multitudes and experience the power of God. And since successful new movements are often launched from an educational base, some of these same new Bible colleges could be the first steps of infant denominations.

The new Boomer churches are known more by their statement of purpose—"How we will minister"—than by their doctrine. Remember that Boomers will cross barriers of doctrinal deviation before they will cross hypocrisy barriers. Boomers want to identify with churches that reflect their nature, that is, winners who are functional, up-to-date and technological. They will join churches that have discovered new ways to communicate the truth of the gospel. And when these churches articulate their methods, they will join other churches of like ministry style.

The old buzz words of denominational understanding among churches were "like faith," meaning doctrine, and "like practice," meaning life-style. The new passion is for "like ministry."

The day of the denomination is not dead, but denominations are changing the way they play the game. The new day of the denomination emphasizes moving toward a community of churches that are of like function and ministry.

18
SUMMARY AND CONCLUSION

M ANY COMPARISONS CAN BE MADE AMONG THE CHURCHES IN THIS book. For example, six of the pastors are Boomer pastors—Maxwell, Hybels, Pope, Galloway, Cotton and MacIntosh. The other pastors were born in pre-Boomer days.

Methodology

In my opinion, five of the churches described here are traditional churches with innovative methods—First Baptist of Jacksonville, Second Baptist of Houston, Central Community Church of Wichita, Mount Paran Church of God in Atlanta and Skyline Wesleyan Church in San Diego. The other five churches are innovative in nature.

Four of the churches were planted by the current pastor, meaning that it was relatively easy to be innovative. These pastors are Pope, Hybels, Galloway and MacIntosh. The other six pastors took over a traditional church and made changes. We can therefore observe two styles of leadership in this book: The founding pastor who can innovate change more easily than the pastor who has been called to a traditional church; the pastor who has had to deal with the old before he can plant the new.

Theology

Four of the churches are Calvinistic in theological orientation—Perimeter, Willow Creek, First Baptist of Jacksonville and Second Baptist of Houston. Six are Wesleyan and/or Arminian—Skyline, New Hope Community, The Church On The Way, Mount Paran, Horizon Christian Fellowship and Central Community.

Location

All of the churches are urban in their outlook, even though some are located in the suburbs instead of the downtown area. The Walrath City-church types don't always apply to these churches. Probably, all are a Type 3—a metropolitan church ministering to the whole metropolitan area.

Two of the churches are located in inner-city-influenced neighborhoods—The Church On The Way and Skyline Wesleyan. These two neighborhoods, however, don't have all the sociological appearances of an inner city, with institutional blight and community stagnation. One of the churches, First Baptist of Jacksonville, is located in a downtown area.

Two of the traditional churches have changed locations since the pastor came—Mount Paran and Central Community. Four founding pastors have moved their church locations at least once—Pope at Perimeter Presbyterian, Hybels at Willow Creek, Galloway at New Hope and MacIntosh at Horizon. In analyzing the motives for moving these main campuses, we may note that all four moved from a less-than-desirable neighborhood to acquire more property or to locate in a better area.

Clergy Education

One pastor has an earned Ph.D. Interestingly, he is Paul Walker at

Mount Paran Church of God in Atlanta, which breaks the stereotype many people have that Pentecostals do not pursue higher education. It is interesting that none of the Calvinist pastors have earned doctorates, even though their tradition emphasizes higher education.

Marital Status

Two of the pastors are divorced—Galloway and MacIntosh—and have learned to face their situation honestly without attempts to hide it. Both have allowed their experience to give them increased sensitivity for ministering to hurting people. While I would not agree with ordaining a divorced person to the ministry, I recognize that God has used ministers who disagreed with my views in other areas, such as baptism, sign-gifts and the second blessing. Even though I am personally committed to a dispensational view of Bible interpretation, I recognize the "law of blessability"—God blesses commitment, prayer and the preaching of the fundamentals of the faith.

God has chosen to bless Galloway and MacIntosh because of their dedication to Him. Over 5,000 people listen to each of them preach His Word every week. God never blesses doctrinal orthodoxy alone. Although He cannot bless less than orthodoxy or the denial of orthodoxy, He blesses more than orthodoxy.

Saturday Night Worship

Perhaps the most controversial innovation in this book is the Saturday night worship service at Willow Creek Community Church. As I mention this practice of Bill Hybels in my seminars, I get outwardly negative reactions. Some people simply don't like it. They feel that worship must be on the Lord's Day. I agree with them, but the Boomers are generally just as vocal in supporting the Saturday night service.

This disagreement is typical of other innovations in this book. While they may be subject to argument, their effectiveness is not. As I was describing the Willow Creek service at a pastors conference in New York, a pastor spoke up in disagreement. I responded, "I may agree with you; but if you had 300 people in church on Saturday night, would you preach to them?"

The response of the other pastors in the room was vocal and affirmative: "Yes, we would preach to them!"

APPENDIX

THE STATISTICS IN THE FOLLOWING 12 COMPARATIVE CHARTS WERE SUP-
plied by the 10 churches reviewed in this book, and were
compiled for reliability and accuracy. They are presented for the
serious student who wishes to research, analyze and compare
innovative trends with programs and growth.

Church Membership

	1979	1980	1986	1987	1988	1989
Skyline Wesleyan	1,490	1,457	1,812	2,066	2,125	2,485
Willow Creek Community	N/A	N/A	834	1,019	1,294	1,666
The Church On The Way	2,494	2,903	5,606	6,217	6,752	7,056
New Hope Community	409	515	3,398	4,001	4,651	5,058
Perimeter Church	250	350	1,006	1,273	1,562	1,900
First Baptist	10,214	11,460	16,654	17,711	18,672	19,588
Central Community	550	600	1,200	1,400	1,575	3,050
Second Baptist	4,563	5,128	10,481	12,410	13,733	15,064
Horizon Christian Fellowship	DOES NOT HAVE OFFICIAL MEMBERSHIP					
Mount Paran Church of God	4,141	4,691	8,679	9,240	9,464	9,825

Average Worship Attendance

	1979	1980	1986	1987	1988	1989
Skyline Wesleyan	1,040	1,133	2,265	2,566	2,901	3,128
Willow Creek Community	1,898	2,057	6,980	8,656	10,346	12,002
The Church On The Way	3,268	3,649	4,922	5,383	5,358	5,347
New Hope Community	400	500	3,400	4,000	4,500	5,000
Perimeter Church	300	450	1,200	1,425	1,745	2,000
First Baptist	3,700	4,100	6,600	6,800	7,000	7,600
Central Community	510	550	1,107	1,283	1,380	2,015
Second Baptist	1,888	2,104	7,907	10,260	11,240	12,182
Horizon Christian Fellowship	1,900	2,000	2,500	3,200	3,500	3,800
Mount Paran Church of God	3,231	3,659	6,769	7,209	8,030	8,850

Average Sunday School Attendance

	1979	1980	1986	1987	1988	1989
Skyline Wesleyan	1,326	1,355	1,865	2,098	2,452	2,596
Willow Creek Community	405	478	2,279	3,107	3,369	4,112
The Church On The Way	1,474	1,582	1,447	1,989	2,053	2,148
New Hope Community	200	250	800	1,000	1,200	1,500
Perimeter Church	250	300	850	1,000	1,100	1,290
First Baptist	3,551	3,979	5,388	5,690	5,944	6,272
Central Community	514	600	921	1,000	1,100	1,250
Second Baptist	948	1,105	4,091	4,386	4,804	5,193
Horizon Christian Fellowship	N/A	N/A	N/A	N/A	N/A	N/A
Mount Paran Church of God	1,180	1,247	1,424	1,682	1,741	1,906

Average Children's Sunday School Attendance

	1979	1980	1986	1987	1988	1989
Skyline Wesleyan	483	498	637	771	854	861
Willow Creek Community	172	221	1,046	1,524	1,734	2,074
The Church On The Way	693	743	839	1,029	1,045	1,025
New Hope Community	N/A	N/A	N/A	N/A	N/A	N/A
Perimeter Church	80	100	280	300	330	400
First Baptist	1,017	1,034	1,408	1,480	1,567	1,682
Central Community	N/A	N/A	N/A	N/A	N/A	N/A
Second Baptist	211	241	767	857	911	973
Horizon Christian Fellowship	850	875	950	950	1,000	1,200
Mount Paran Church of God	492	523	560	679	759	898

Average Attendance of Youth in Sunday School

	1979	1980	1986	1987	1988	1989
Skyline Wesleyan	265	254	243	243	267	261
Willow Creek Community	757	715	1,050	900	950	1,350
The Church On The Way	192	206	221	240	257	270
New Hope Community	N/A	N/A	N/A	N/A	N/A	N/A
Perimeter Church	30	39	60	80	110	140
First Baptist	522	547	607	666	680	694
Central Community	N/A	N/A	N/A	N/A	N/A	N/A
Second Baptist	94	116	330	359	396	444
Horizon Christian Fellowship	MIDWEEK STUDIES ONLY					150
Mount Paran Church of God	110	132	184	212	170	178

Average Attendance of Adults in Sunday School

	1979	1980	1986	1987	1988	1989
Skyline Wesleyan	465	489	727	825	988	1,141
Willow Creek Community	405	478	2,279	3,107	3,369	4,112
The Church On The Way	589	633	387	720	751	853
New Hope Community	N/A	N/A	N/A	N/A	N/A	N/A
Perimeter Church	140	161	510	520	660	750
First Baptist	1,907	2,474	3,326	3,350	3,817	3,933
Central Community	N/A	N/A	N/A	N/A	N/A	N/A
Second Baptist	643	748	2,994	3,170	3,497	3,776
Horizon Christian Fellowship	DOES NOT HAVE ADULT SUNDAY CLASSES					
Mount Paran Church of God	578	592	680	791	812	830

Income

	1979	1980	1986	1987	1988	1989
Skyline Wesleyan	694K	753K	1.98M	2.32M	2.37M	3.87M
Willow Creek Community	1.26M	1.33M	5.5M	7.84M	8.16M	10.59M
The Church On The Way	3.7M	4.7M	7.8M	9.0M	11.1M	11.5M
New Hope Community	268K	327K	1.57M	1.87M	2.0M	2.25M
Perimeter Church	300K	380K	1.9M	2.5M	3.0M	3.3M
First Baptist	2.98M	3.67M	7.15M	9.42M	10.32M	9.44M
Central Community	365K	440K	2.23K	1.51M	2.0M	2.0M
Second Baptist	1.5M	1.98M	10.62M	9.7M	14.0M	12.8M
Horizon Christian Fellowship	N/A	N/A	1.6M	2.1M	2.5M	2.9M
Mount Paran Church of God	1.74M	2.31M	5.09M	7.0M	10.08M	10.9M

K—denotes thousand

M—denotes million

Number of Conversions

	1979	1980	1986	1987	1988	1989
Skyline Wesleyan	407	519	700	793	856	916
Willow Creek Community	N/A	N/A	N/A	N/A	N/A	N/A
The Church On The Way	2,547	2,090	1,950	2,070	2,340	3,436
New Hope Community	80%	80%	80%	80%	80%	80%
Perimeter Church	19	23	59	38	55	70
First Baptist	1,503	1,477	1,343	1,414	1,240	1,186
Central Community	N/A	N/A	N/A	N/A	227	363
Second Baptist	161	149	766	838	797	815
Horizon Christian Fellowship	690	700	720	825	820	850
Mount Paran Church of God	373	426	543	568	716	883

Number of Baptisms

	1979	1980	1986	1987	1988	1989
Skyline Wesleyan	87	102	143	135	203	146
Willow Creek Community	N/A	N/A	614	465	620	627
The Church On The Way	843	870	983	964	788	781
New Hope Community	N/A	N/A	N/A	N/A	N/A	N/A
Perimeter Church	19	24	72	83	68	88
First Baptist	938	1,067	974	950	915	879
Central Community	N/A	N/A	N/A	N/A	40	48
Second Baptist	142	123	652	701	655	767
Horizon Christian Fellowship	590	620	625	650	690	767
Mount Paran Church of God	80	91	159	129	165	254

	Building Value	Seating Capacity	Acreage Attached to Church	Parking Spaces	Denomina- tion	Cell Groups/# Attendance
Skyline Wesleyan	4,334,355	1,144	8.3	450 on site	Wesleyan	Yes/96 ------- 1,135
Willow Creek Community	12.3M	4,554	127	2,650	Interdenomi- national	Yes/251 ------- 1,800
The Church On The Way	25M	4,000[1]	20	1,850[2]	International Church of the Foursquare Gospel [3]	Yes/79 ------- 1,000
New Hope Community	10M	3,000	41	1,150	Non-Denomi- national	Yes/500 ------- 4,800
Perimeter Church	6,500,000	1,100	110	Not Given	Presbyterian Church in America	Yes/120 ------- 1,600
First Baptist	47,000,000	3,500	9 Blocks	3,265[4]	Southern Baptist	No -------
Central Community	10,600,900	3,200	57.2	988 paved	Church of God Ander- son	Yes/65-70 ------- 850
Second Baptist	90,000,000	6,200	48	4,887[5]	Southern Baptist	No -------
Horizon Christian Fellowship	N/A	1,950	20	N/A	Christian Non-Denomi- national	Yes/90 ------- 1,800
Mount Paran Church of God	Central 14M North 12.1M	Central 2,200 North 3,500	Central 14.6 North 65	Central 832 North 1,250 Bus 1,110	Church of God	Yes/270[6] ------- 2,500

(1) 2400 E. Campus/1600 W. Campus   (2) 700 E. Campus, 500 W. Campus, Satellite 650   (3) Interna-tional Church of the Foursquare Gospel "Deaconing"   (4) 2,536 owned by church - 729 others available   (5) 2,387 on campus, 2,500 off campus   (6) 120 Fellowship groups/150 Vine Life groups

	Tape Ministry Audio/ Video	Television Ministry #of Stations	Radio Ministry #of Stations	Outreach Program Plan Followed	# of Visits Per Week # Involved
Skyline Wesleyan	YES Audio	NO	NO	Yes/G.R.A.D.E. Growth Resulting after Discipleship & Evangelisim 4 large groups	250
Willow Creek Community	YES Audio	NO	NO	Yes/Weekend outreach team responds to reqest for contact	70 35
The Church On The Way	YES Audio/ Video	YES *1012	YES 160	Yes/Various community service & evangelistic	N/A
New Hope Community	YES Audio	NO	NO	Yes/ N/A	13,000 500 Lay Pastors
Perimeter Church	YES Audio	NO	N/A	NO	NO
First Baptist	YES Audio/ Video	YES 1	YES 2	Yes/Inreach ministry to members & outreach to prospects through S.S. Dept/Class Organization	3,000 1,500
Central Community	YES Audio/ Video	YES 1	NO	Yes/Phone calling follow-up by T.L.C. Groups	N/A
Second Baptist	YES Audio/ Video	YES 123+CBN, TBN	YES 1	Yes/Supper outreach Mon. & Tues. evenings by Sun. School Class	200-250 723
Horizon Christian Fellowship	YES Audio/ Video	YES	YES 14	Yes/Team evangelism street min. & outreach local, national, international	Records not kept
Mount Paran Church of God	YES Audio/ Video	YES 3	YES 16	Yes/Personal Witness training; Elders, 1st time visitor; Vine Life Phone Min. Pastoral Visit.	125,200+ phone calls 72

*TBN serves 200, 800 cable outlets; more than a dozen independent

	K-12 Day School - - - - - - # Enrolled	Post High School/ College	Name of School	# of Students	Purpose of School
Skyline Wesleyan	NO	NO			
Willow Creek Community	NO	NO			
The Church On The Way	NO	YES	The King's Institute	300	Foster personal growth, enhance min. of members, prepare people for ministry
New Hope Community	NO	NO			
Perimeter Church	Grades 1-8 - - - - - - 150	NO			
First Baptist	NO	NO			
Central Community	NO	NO			
Second Baptist	YES - - - - - - 965	NO			
Horizon Christian Fellowship	Pre thru 10 - - - - - - 400	YES	Horizon School of Evangelism	75	Equipping believers for evangelism
Mount Paran Church of God	YES - - - - - - 675	YES	Psychological Studies Institute	75	Graduate program offers M.S. w/ major in community counseling at Georgia State Univ.; ecumenical program housed at Mount Paran